Take Off Your Shoes

You're Standing on Holy Ground

Anne Dier Wilson

Take Off Your Shoes © 2012 by Anne Dier Wilson
Shoe Therapy © 2012 by Lenora Nazworth

Published by Volunteers of America of North Louisiana
360 Jordan St.
Shreveport, La. 71101
www.voanorthla.org

Book and cover design by Danielle Richard
Editorial consultant: Marilyn Joiner

ISBN: 978-0-615-66100-1

Printed in the United States of America

FOREWORD

This book is gifted with a deep sense of God's Presence.

So rather than reading it as I intended, as a Daily Devotional, I found myself being drawn forward, page by page, lifted and grateful. Anne Wilson's radiant faith, lucid prose, and wide erudition constantly help the reader experience God.

There is something of a paradox here. For her, real awareness of God comes not so much from others' words, even if theologically true, as from responding personally to His will, which we know from Jesus of Nazareth. "The way we love our neighbor," she affirms, "is the way we measure our love for God."

Yet reading her words, we find ourselves opening to the God of love! The paradox is melted - by Grace?

So we can join her and the Psalmist (Ps 91) in knowing for ourselves that *"He who dwells in the secret place of the Most High shall abide under the shadow of the Almighty."*

And she emphasizes "abide": this experience need not be fleeting or rare. She even gently rebuts a dear one's warning that one cannot live on the mountaintop: quite the reverse - *"Where shall I go from your spirit? Or where shall I flee from your presence? (Ps 139)."*

We're on the mountain, it is God's mountain, and we hear His voice! Many faithful people, to ensure we are not deceiving ourselves or others about such "super-natural" claims as a personal experience of the Spirit, or hearing a Divine voice, apply certain wise tests.

First and foremost we ask, can this experience be confirmed by the weight of Scripture?

Second, by reason, by the brains God gave us and expects us to use? True, His ways are not ours, but a redeemed mind can make a sensible interpretation of God's truth.

Third, by tradition? By what has been foundational from the beginnings of the church, and in accord with the best understandings of the faithful over these past two millennia.

And fourth, by experience in our personal and communal journey of faith?

In all four, Anne convinces me: such that even in her moments of seeking Him, she is finding Him.

Finally - also as a good Methodist - she methodically identifies both those actions and attitudes which often prevent our awareness of God's Presence, and then those that actively help us truly dwell in Him.

-- How lifting it is to experience this close, unbroken oneness with our Life-Giver!

It is, as Wesley said, the best of all.

God is with us!

~Donald A. Webb.

INTRODUCTION

O just Father, the world has not known You, but I have, Joy, Joy, Joy, tears of Joy. - Pascal [1]

It was a feeling of emptiness that I sensed as I talked with an attractive young Swedish girl who sat next to me on a flight from Stockholm to New York. When we took our seats on the plane, we introduced ourselves and started talking about how beautiful the city was, all decorated for the Christmas season. I told her I especially loved the lighted candelabra in all the windows and the real snow dazzling on the trees outside. I told her that coming from the Deep South in the United States, being in snowy Stockholm at Christmas was quite an experience. When I asked her about their celebration of Christmas, she told me that the only time she ever went to church was on Christmas Day. In fact, she said, no one goes to church in Sweden anymore, except on Christmas. They've given it up! As we visited, my heart went out to her. She seemed so spiritually empty. She had no conception of God. In fact, after talking to her, I don't think she had a clue why she even went to church on Christmas Day.

My question is this: how can one give up church, or even more poignant, how can one give up God? Imagine waking up each morning without the awareness of His presence with you?

How sad and empty one must feel not knowing the joy of having

---

[1] Blaise Pascal by Marvin O'Connell   Eerdmans Publishing Company, Grand Rapids, MI 1997

Him right there with you, as close as the air you breathe. To me, it would be like living life in the heart of darkness, with no light at all.

How I thank God for the circumstances, the people, the anything and everything that played a part in connecting me with Him. How frightening it is that I could have lived my life without knowing Him, just like that young Swedish girl. How wonderful and exciting it was when I realized to my amazement that as eagerly as I wanted God in my life, He wanted me even more.

Dedication

I dedicate this book to my granddaughter and namesake, Anne Alexandra Wilson (Allie), to whom I promised years ago I would write it.

One cold, snowy night in Crested Butte, Colorado I was having dinner with my son, Barry, and his three children. They had been skiing all day and Tanner, his oldest son, was so excited because he had done a super job skiing down one of the hardest slopes. During the meal our conversation turned to life's accomplishments. I guess it was the skiing that sparked the conversation, because both boys, Peyton and Tanner, were eager to learn all they could about skiing so they could scale the most difficult slopes. My son, who is an airline pilot for Continental Airlines, told us his goal had been to fly the 777 and after perservering for many years he had accomplished that. They looked at me and said, "Gran, what about you? What is the biggest accomplishment in your life?" Without hesitation I said that far and above all others, the greatest accomplishment in my life is my relationship with God and that relationship gives me great joy and satisfaction. When we finished eating and were leaving the restaurant, Allie, the oldest child and only girl, nestled close to me and whispered, "Granny, I want what you have! I want that kind of relationship with God. How do I get it?" I promised her then that I would write her a letter. Originally, this book started out as a letter that I called "Dear Allie." My prayer is that through this endeavor

I may in someway help her and others connect with God in an intimate and dynamic way.

Also, I dedicate this book to the unknown Swedish girl, who, like the Unknown Soldier, represents a myriad of others just like her.

SOLI DEO GLORIA!

WITH APPRECIATION

First to my son, Paul, who went beyond the call of duty to help me operate and understand the computer that I used while writing this manuscript. Without his loving patience, I would never have gotten it done. Also, to Dr. Tom Siskron for his valuable and always willing assistance. To my daughter, Mary Kathleen, and my good friend, Reverend Ed Dilworth, with whom I shared ideas and who gave me much coveted advice. To my son, Woody, my daughter Roxanne, Marilyn Joiner, and Diane Libro who joined together to edit my manuscript. To Danielle Richard, my graphic artist, who patiently and lovingly put the book together in exactly the way I wanted it to look. To my husband, Woody, my sister, Bonnie, my son, Barry, and my daughter-in-law, Amy, with love and thanks for always being there and encouraging me. Lastly, to Mrs. Z.T. Gallion, (the "old lady" on the tall kitchen stool) who made me know that experiencing God 24/7 was indeed a reality! Without her this book might never have been written.

Take Off Your Shoes

PART I:
Take Off Your Shoes

Earth's crammed with heaven,
and every common bush afire with God,
but only those who see take off their shoes.

Elizabeth Barrett Browning

Holy, holy, holy, is the Lord of hosts; the whole earth is full of His glory. (Isaiah 6:3)[2]

GOAL: To help us become more acutely aware of the holiness of the ordinary. To help us learn to live, move, and have our being in the presence of God; every minute, of every hour, of every day.

In the Old Testament God made His presence evident to two men and actually told them to take off their shoes because they were in His presence and were standing on Holy Ground. The first was Moses, as he stood looking at the burning bush that would not be consumed. And second was Joshua, just before he went into the battle of Jericho. The first is from Exodus Chapter 3:2-5.

And the angel of the Lord appeared unto him in a flame of fire out of the midst of a bush; and he looked, and, behold, the bush burned with fire, and the bush was not consumed.

And Moses said, I will now turn aside and see this great sight, why the bush is not burnt.

And when the Lord saw that he turned aside to see, God called unto him out of the midst of the bush, and said, Moses, Moses. And he said, here am I.

And he said, Draw not near here: put off thy shoes from off thy feet, for the place whereon thou standest is holy ground. (Doesn't it sound like God is saying to Moses, don't leave, take off your shoes and stay awhile)?

The second is Joshua 5:13-15, and it is one of my favorite scriptures.

---

[2] Unless otherwise stated all Scripture citation is from the New Scofield Reference Bible printed in the text of the Authorized King JamesVersion of 1611 - but with word changes.

And it came to pass, when Joshua was by Jericho, that he lifted up his eyes and looked and, behold, there stood a man over against him with his sword drawn in his hand; and Joshua went unto him, and said unto him, Art thou for us, or for our adversaries?

And he said, Nay, but as captain of the host of the Lord am I now come. And Joshua fell on his face to the earth, and did worship, and said unto him, What saith my lord unto his servant?

And the captain of the Lord's host said unto Joshua, Loose thy shoe from off thy foot, for the place whereon thou standest is holy. And Joshua did so.

Have you ever wondered why God told them to take off their shoes? What is the significance of bare feet? Just for a moment I want us to think about how it feels when we take off our shoes. Imagine with me if you will: it's the end of a very busy, frustrating day. You've been running around all day, your feet are tired and hurting, maybe even swollen, and at last you are home and you can take those shoes off, wiggle your toes and relax. How wonderful it feels to be comfortable and relaxed! Freed, not only from the pressure of the shoes, but also from the pressures of the world. Could it be that God also calls us to take off our shoes in His Presence, asking us to stop our busyness, our running around, and just relax in Him? Freeing ourselves from the pressures of the world, we take off our shoes, wiggle our toes, settle down, and just spend time with Him. Luxuriate in His comfort. Relax, be content, and enjoy His company. One of my very favorite devotion books is "31 Days Of Praise" by

Ruth Meyers. She writes, "How delighted I am to have You as my dwelling place where I can settle down, feel secure and be content anywhere on earth - where I can enter and be at rest even when all around and above is a sea of trouble."[3]

Psalm 46:1-3 reads: *God is our refuge and strength, a very present help in trouble. Therefore will not we fear, though the earth be removed, and though the mountains be carried into the midst of the sea; Though the waters thereof roar and be troubled, though the mountains shake with the swelling thereof.*

This scripture tells us that God is a very present help in trouble. He is always present, ready to help us. In His presence, we never again have to be afraid or feel alone.

Romans 8:35-39 says there is nothing that can separate us from our awesome God and His love and protection.

What shall separate us from the love of Christ? Shall tribulation, or distress, or persecution, or famine, or nakedness, or peril, or the sword?

As it is written, for Thy sake we are killed all the day long; we are accounted as sheep for the slaughter.

Nay, in all these things we are more than conquerors through Him that loved us.

For I am persuaded that neither death, nor life, nor angels, nor principalities, nor powers, nor things present, nor things to come,

Nor height, nor depth, nor any other creation, shall be able to separate us from the love of God, which is in Christ Jesus, our

---

[3] 31 Days of Praise by Ruth Meyers, p 86 Multnomah Publishers Inc., Sisters, Oregon, 1994.

Lord.

This is a wonderful and mighty promise! It seems to cover the whole spectrum of things that could possibly separate us from God. And it says that none of them can do it. I know it's true and I believe it with all my heart. But do I experience it? There is a vast difference between believing something and experiencing it. I have to confess there are times in my life that I do feel separated from God and His love. And my question is, "Why"? I long, I yearn, I hunger to be ever aware of God's presence with me, as did Brother Lawrence, a monk, who more than 300 years ago, wrote an intriguing little book called, "The Practice of the Presence of God."[4] As I read it, I knew from experience some of things he was talking about, and it whetted my appetite to know more, so that I could more deeply experience God's presence with me all the time.

In his book Brother Lawrence addresses this very subject. He said that the most essential ingredient of the Christian life is this: how to remain in the presence of God all the time; every minute of every hour of every day. John Wesley also experienced this awesome awareness of God's presence with him. On his death bed he said, "The best of all, God is with us!"[5] The awareness that God was with him was the center, the very essence of his faith and life. Knowing that God is with us should also be the center of our faith and life. The apostle Paul put it this way in Acts 17:28: *For in him we live, and move, and have our being.* This knowledge, I believe is what gives us that abundant life, pressed down, overflowing with joy unspeakable

---

[4] The Practice of the Presence of God by Brother Lawrence Whitaker House, Springdale, PA, 1982.
[5] Last Words of Saints and Sinners by Herbert Lockyer, p.65 Kregel Publication, Grand Rapids, MI 1969

and peace that passes all understanding that Jesus promised us. It's what lifts us up on eagles' wings when we are down. This is our heritage! I believe that Jesus meant for each one of us to have it, to be totally aware of it all the time. It should be the most real thing in the whole world to us. It should be the norm for all Christians. I love this poem by Ralph Cushman because it says it so succinctly:

Life is worthwhile, dear God, To those who know This rich companionship with Thee; Each morning as the day flames forth, Each evening in a sweet Tranquility. Ten million gifts Spring from Thy hand, Of up-flung mountains, evening skies, a tree! Yet never one can quite compare with this - the giving of Thyself to me! [6]

We all know that there are literally millions of blessings and gifts that God pours out upon each of us every day of our life. He is so extravagant in His love for us. Just look around at the world that He has created for our pleasure. The sun, the moon, the stars, the sky, the oceans, the lakes, the mountains, the trees, the flowers - not to mention our families, our grandchildren, our friends, our homes. But of all these multitudinous blessings that He gives us, nothing can even begin to compare to the blessing of His Presence in our lives.

"He Lives" is one of my very favorite songs, and it says it so wonderfully:

I serve a risen savior, he's in the world today. I know that he is living, whatever men may say. I see his hand of mercy, I hear his voice of cheer and just the time I need him, He's always near. He lives, he lives, Christ Jesus lives today. He walks with me

---

[6] Practicing the Presence by Ralph Cushman, p 47, Abingdon Press, Nashville, Tennessee 1936

and talks with me along life's narrow way. He lives, he lives, Christ Jesus lives today. You ask me how I know he lives, he lives within my heart.[7]

I don't know about you, but I desperately yearn for the awareness of this extraordinary treasure, this gift of gifts, God's very presence with me all the time. Not just happenstance, not just every once in a while, not just when I'm inspired when the choir leads us in beautiful praise and worship, not just when I'm awestruck at seeing a beautiful sunset, not just when I feel like falling on my face at seeing the majesty and glory and intricacy of His handiwork. I want to feel His presence with me when I'm going down a muddy road in life and I get stuck in a ditch, with no cell phone to call for help. I want to be totally aware that He is beside me when everything in my life seems to be falling apart and nothing makes sense. I want to feel Him there when my child is going through a horrendous divorce, and I have to stand by in the mud and watch as hatred sets in like cancer. I want to feel Him there when a grandchild loses her way and can't seem to get back on track. I want to feel Him with me when the diagnosis is bad and when death comes. I want to feel Him with me in the downs, as well as in the ups, and know with assurance that when I do get knocked down, I will never have to stay there. I want to feel His presence all the time – no matter what. I want to know that He is as close as the breath I breathe. I want to know this without a single doubt in my mind. I want to feel that God is by my side, as near as the air that I am breathing. I want to know that as sure as the sun arises each morning, that's how sure I am that He's with me. I want to

---

[7] He Lives by Alfred Ackley, p 310, The United Methodist Hymnal, The United Methodist Publishing House, Nashville, TN1989

experience that!

From reading and studying the scriptures, I believe that living in the presence of God, being fully aware that we are in His presence should be the most normal thing that happens to a Christian. I think it is interesting that I have gone to church all my life (since I was a baby), and I have heard very few sermons that address this subject directly. Brother Lawrence said that if he had been a preacher, (he actually worked in the kitchen at the monastery) every sermon that he preached would have been on this very subject: Always being aware of living in God's presence.

For many years I did not know that actually living moment by moment in God's presence was even a possibility. Trust me, it doesn't just happen (anyway, not in my life). I went to church all my life, beginning when I was on the cradle roll. I went every Sunday morning and every Sunday night. I went to Wednesday night Prayer meeting and in between I went to Girl's Auxiliary. But it was not until the summer that I was almost fourteen years old, that I actually experienced the awareness of God's presence with me for the first time. It happened one evening while I was at church camp.

We had gone down to the banks of Lake Pontchartrain for vespers and were sitting there overlooking that incredibly beautiful lake. I suddenly felt an overwhelming sense of God being with me. It was so wonderful! (Up to this point in my life there was only a fuzzy image in my mind regarding God). I had been taught that when I died I would go to heaven and God would be there and I would be with Him forever. But after feeling His awesome presence with me on Lake Pontchartrain it made me realize that I really didn't have to die and go to heaven to be with Him. On that day my appetite was whetted for

God! I desired to live in His presence all the time. How wonderful it was going to be to live each day of my life knowing that He was with me.

    I couldn't wait until I got home to tell my minister, who was also my older brother and fresh out of seminary. I told him what had happened at camp and that I wanted to live in God's presence all the time and be aware that He was always with me. I then asked him, "Tell me how I can do it"? He said to me, "Anne, you can't. It's impossible. That was a mountaintop experience you had and you can't live your life on top of a mountain. You have to live in the valley." Sadly, I left his office, believing he was right. That is why it is important that we know what the scriptures say for ourselves, so that we don't have to depend on somebody else's knowledge of them. Had I been a more mature Christian, steeped in God's Word, I would have known that what I was told was simply not true. That is why it is imperative that we study and know what the Scriptures say for ourselves. Second Timothy 2:15 reads: *Study to show yourself approved unto God, a workman that need not be ashamed, rightly dividing the word of truth.*

    After this experience, I kept on going to church and reading my Bible every day, but seldom experiencing the intense joy I felt at camp that summer. Years passed. I went to college, and right after graduating, I got married, and two years later I had a baby. One morning I was at home with the baby, and as I stood looking out the window, I was once again surprised by Joy, and felt that wonderful presence of God with me. It was exhilarating! I knew without a doubt I was in His presence and I loved it. I thanked Him and told Him that it was my earnest desire, my great yearning to live in His presence all the time. (I made it very clear that I did not mean I wanted to die and go to heaven to accomplish this; after all, I had a baby to raise)!

We had moved to Shreveport by this time and joined Noel Memorial United Methodist Church. One Sunday I got the baby dressed and we went to Sunday School and Church. Since I had a baby, I decided that the logical place to go to Sunday School was the Mother's Class; a decision I found out later was totally orchestrated by God, (remember what I had prayed)? I went into this class where I knew no one. The teacher was an older woman - seriously old - who sat on one of those tall kitchen stools as she taught. (As I reflect, I'm sure she was probably in her seventies, but at my tender age of twenty-four she looked to me to be around a hundred). I took a seat and as she began to speak, I was totally and completely surprised. I couldn't believe what I was hearing. She knew God in a capacity that no one I had ever met in my whole life knew Him.

She talked like He was her best friend and not only that, He was right there on that kitchen stool with her. I have no clue what she said. It wasn't important. God was there with her and that was all I needed to know. After the class ended I went up to her and said , "I don't know you and you don't know me, but I am not going to let you get away from me until I find out how you got to know God the way you do."

When I walked out of that classroom, for the first time in my life, I knew it was possible to live in the presence of God. I had seen it firsthand. At the same time that I had prayed my heartfelt prayer that I wanted to live in His presence; God had laid it on this lady's heart to teach a group of women in her home once a week. For the next seven years she taught this little group of twelve young women. It was a very serious Bible Study. We did not have cookies, juice and a lot of socializing. We were there for one purpose: to study God's word. We started the sessions with singing and praising and spent the rest of the time with our heads in the Bible. We started with the Pentateuch and ended with the Gospel of Mark. That was it. But in those seven years we were fed. Our spiritual bodies that we received when we became Christians began to grow and mature. One of our first assignments was to memorize Psalm 91. The first verse says: *He who dwells in the secret place of the Most High, shall abide under the shadow of the Almighty.* Had it not been for that "old lady" on the kitchen stool and her obedience when God asked her to teach that class, I probably never would have learned to live my life in the shadow of the Almighty.

"Take Off Your Shoes" will hopefully make us more aware of God's presence with us and help us abide always in His shadow. We will explore reasons that may block this awareness and also try to find ways to help us become more aware of His presence with us.

Now, surprisingly, just as desperately as we want God in our lives, He wants us in His life even more. It's mind-boggling to think that the God of the Universe wants us in His presence and eagerly waits for us to come to Him. Remember the scripture we just read in Exodus. When God saw that Moses was going to turn aside, and He said to him, "Moses, don't do that; take off your shoes and stay awhile." In John 12:32 we are told that God even draws us to Himself: *And I, if I am lifted up from the earth, will draw all men unto to me.* And in James 4:8 it says, *Draw near to God, and He will draw near to you.* Jesus knew how important it was for us to abide in God's presence constantly. In fact, He thought it was so important, that He prayed for it to happen the very night He was arrested. Not once, not twice, not three times, but four times He repeated that prayer in John 17: *That they may be one, as you Father, are in Me and I in You, that they may also be one in us.* That prayer was not just for His disciples. In verse 20 of the same chapter, Jesus says, *"Neither pray I for these alone, but for them also who shall believe on Me though their word."* Jesus prayed this prayer for each and every one of us! So I believe that we can drive a stake in that promise, we can lay claim to it. We can say unequivocally, this is our heritage, this is the way it was meant to be, because Jesus asked Father God to make it possible when He prayed for us.

Oh, loving Father show us how we can live with You in this capacity all the time!

Take Off Your Shoes

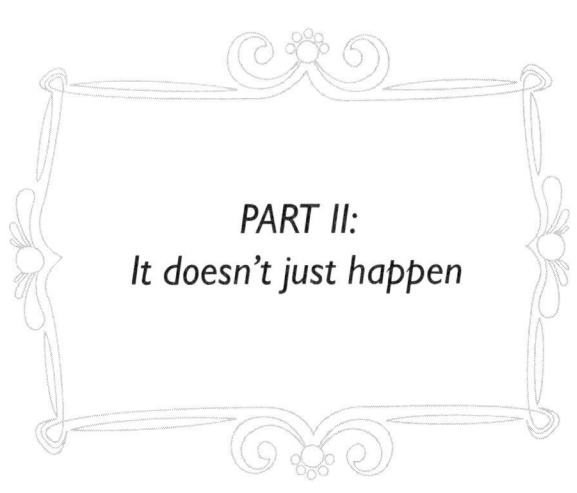

PART II:
It doesn't just happen

Seek the Lord and His strength;

seek his presence continually

Psalm 105:4

*A*ll Christians start with the same premise, though as we grow spiritually, we find ourselves on different levels. We've either given our life to Jesus, been saved, been strangely warmed, been born again, been confirmed - whichever way we express it. In other words, our religion is not hearsay. We've all had a personal encounter with God and given our lives to Him. And at that time He imparted to each of us His Spirit so that we might be able to experience Him and communicate with Him. He gave us spiritual eyes to see Him and spiritual ears to hear Him. Because of what the Scriptures tell us, we have the capacity to be one with the God of the universe all the time, just as Jesus prayed for it to happen. And we've all experienced this oneness, this special contact with God at one time or hopefully many times, or even better all the time. (There are exceptions, like this seventy year old man in my Sunday School Class who told me he had never once felt God's presence with him. He has been going to church all his life).

After we have felt God's presence with us, our appetites have been whetted for Him. We are hungry for Him. We want this wonderful experience all the time. As it says in Psalm 91, we are to abide under His shadow. Abide means always and continuous. But my big problem is that I am not consistent, constant, always, continuously abiding in Him. I'm like a firefly on a summer night – off and on, on and off. Brother Lawrence said, we have joy, then sadness; peace, then anxiety; confidence then heaviness. I hope you are not like that. I hate that happenstance, fleeting awareness of His presence with me. It is so frustrating. Once we've experienced His presence with us, we feel bereft; we feel a great void in our lives when we are not aware of

Him. Once we've known and felt His presence with us we are not only dissatisfied, we are miserable to live without this awareness of Him. And once we've experienced this oneness, He will not let us be content with a lower level of fellowship with Him.

I believe He allows us to be miserable until we are drawn back to Him. We can be content with nothing less than knowing God in all His majesty and being aware of His loving presence throughout each day.

This prayer by Ralph Cushman expresses it perfectly:

Eternal God, we join the innumerable company of those who seek your heart. But we have sought before; we have sought and then forsaken you. The world of things has called and we have left the path that leads to you, until sometimes we have even doubted if you are. But something in the depths of us keeps calling us back until we doubt our doubts. And we doubt our doubts because we know that when we close our minds to you the lights go out, the skies sink down, life grows so barren, joyless and dead! Oh Father God we cannot do without you and yet so often you do seem so far away. Oh bring your dwelling place closer to our own. We want a closer walk with you, we want an acute awareness of your presence with us all the time. Help us to believe it's possible - not because of our knowledge of you - but because of the nearness of you. [8]

And just as the prayer says, we've got to believe it's possible. We don't want to be like the little boy who lost something very dear to him. He looked and looked for it, to no avail. Finally, his mother told

---

8   Practicing the Presence, pp 16,40 (Adapted from two prayers by Ralph Cushman)

him he should pray about it and ask God to help him find it. He told her he had already asked God to help him find it. He said God told him He had looked for it and couldn't find it either. He said it was just totally lost! In Mark 9:23 Jesus says, *"If you can believe, all things are possible to him that believes."*

This problem of a happenstance relationship is not unique with us or our time. As far back as Revelation 2:4-5 Jesus tells the church at Ephesus, *"I have somewhat against you, because you have left your first love. Remember therefore from where you have fallen and repent and do the first works."* Ralph Cushman, in his book "The Practice of the Presence of God," said it seems the first works for a Christian is maintaining the glow of our first love for Christ - which means keeping alive the consciousness of His Presence.[9] Do you remember when you first fell in love? Did you think about that person very much? Did even the thought of that person make you exceedingly happy and excited? I think that's what Ralph Cushman is talking about. We need to recapture our first love and excitement for Jesus. We need to think about Him even when we're not praying. But unfortunately a lot of us are experiencing what Hannah Whitall Smith described in her book "The Christian's Secret of a Happy Life."[10] She said that many of us feel about our religion like we do a headache. We don't want to get rid of our head, but it hurts to keep it. God didn't mean for our relationship with Him to hurt. I believe He meant for us to be the happiest, most content, most peaceful people on earth. In order for this to happen, we have to recapture our

---

9   Ralph Cushman, p 114
10 The Christian's Secret of a Happy Life by Hannah Whitall Smith, p.15   Fleming H. Revell Company, Westwood, NJ

first love and enthusiasm for Him.

One time my husband and I were stranded in the Houston airport all day and night because of an ice storm. For hours we sat in the small section of the airport where there was Internet access. As we sat there I noticed this young man next to us who had pulled up a picture of this young woman on his computer. For 15 to 20 minutes he just sat there looking at her picture. Curiosity got the best of me and I asked him if she was his girlfriend. "No," he replied. "She's my wife." I said, "I can tell you really love her." "Hopelessly," he replied. That's first love! So how do we capture it or recapture it? And what is first love anyway?

In the royal command Jesus tells us, *"You shall love the Lord your God with all your heart, and with all your soul, and with all your mind, and with all your strength: this is the first commandment."* (Mark 12:30) Sounds like first love, doesn't it? I think that our idea of loving God is elusive, hard to pin down. How can we really know if we are loving Him or not, especially in this "first love" capacity? If you ask me if I loved God this much, and I said I did, how could you really tell if I were telling the truth or not? There is no way we can see into each other's heart. But God, in his great wisdom, made it possible for us to tell how much we really love Him, in a clear and obvious way. In the very next verse He says, *"And the second is this: You shall love your neighbor as yourself. There is no other commandment greater than these."* (Mark 12:31)

How are we loving our neighbor? (That's something that we can see and hear). The way we love our neighbor, the way we treat our neighbor, is the way we measure our love for God. I have had this precious neighbor for forty-two years. Her name is Susan, and I love her dearly. Do you think Jesus meant that if I loved her as myself, I would have fulfilled that command? That would have been a piece of cake, because Susan is so easy to love. Our "neighbor" is all the people we come in contact with everyday, people that God puts into our lives. How are we loving them? How are we treating them? I think this is what Jesus was trying to get across to Peter in the 21st chapter of John. Remember, Jesus asks Peter three times if he loved Him. Peter replies each time in the affirmative. Then, after each reply, Jesus tells Peter: first, feed My lambs, second, feed my sheep, and third, feed my sheep. It sounds like Jesus was saying to Peter, if you really love me, you can show it by loving and taking care of others. So, I believe the way we love and care for others is the way we measure our love for Jesus.

As I said earlier, we are probably all on different levels in our relationship with God. Relationships are relative. Some of us may be miles ahead and ever conscious of His presence with us. Some of us may be way behind, trying to catch up or even struggling to keep the relationship alive. I like to compare our relationship with God to the tabernacle in the Old Testament.

The word tabernacle actually means to dwell (with God). There was a fence that surrounded the tabernacle and to get inside you had to enter through the gate. When you came in you were automatically in the outer court, then there was the inner court or the holy place. Finally, separated from the holy place by a very thick veil was the Holy of Holies, where God dwelled. In Old Testament times only the most high priest could enter the Holy of Holies, and then only with bells on the hem of his robe to announce his coming in and his going out. Legend has it that a rope was tied to his ankle in case something happened to him while he was in there and they had to pull him out.

In our relationship with God, we have all gotten beyond the fence by entering through the gate or door, which is Jesus. Remember, Jesus told us that He is the door by which we are to enter. In John 10:9 He says, *"I am the door; by me if any man enter in, he shall be saved, and shall go in and out, and find pasture."* As we enter through the gate, we are in the outer court, and maybe some of us have even made it to the next level which is the inner court or holy place. But our goal is to be in the Holy of Holies, where we can live, move, and have our being in the very presence of God forever, starting right now. Psalm 91:4 tells us that it is in this secret place of the Most High that: *He shall cover you with His feathers and under His wings shall you trust.* And I believe it is in the Holy of Holies that God wants us all to be.

How privileged we are that God made this possible for us when He sent Jesus to die for our sins. He closed that gap between Himself and us (that gap between the divine and the human) that had been caused by sin. Remember when Adam and Eve disobeyed in the Garden of Eden? Their sin caused them to be separated from God, just as our sins today cause us to be separated from God. Sin always has, and always will, separate us from God. As Jesus hung on the cross the veil that separated the inner court and the Holy of Holies was torn from top to bottom, so that no longer was just the high priest privileged to go in and be with God, but now we all have that privilege. As mind boggling as it seems, we can now not only enter but run with open arms and actually live there – in His presence, all the time. I'm not talking about life after death; I'm talking about life before death – this very moment!

It is God, Himself, that has put this longing, this desire and this hunger in our hearts to be one with Him. St. Augustine said, He has put a God shaped void in our hearts and we will never be satisfied until that void is filled with Him. My big question is this: Is it within our reach? Is it possible? Frank Laubach posed this question: "Can we be in His presence all the time awake, fall asleep in His arms, and awaken in His presence"? Brother Lawrence said "Yes, it is possible!" He did it. In a very simplistic way, he tells us how he lived out his daily life always aware of being in God's presence. He brought his total life under full surrender to Jesus. He is a wonderful example and role model. He practiced continuously his communion with God until that communion became more than a habit (like brushing his teeth), it became his second nature (like breathing). God was his life! And wherever he went he carried with him the consciousness of God's presence. He could have written the following verses from Psalm 139:7-10.

Where shall I go from your spirit? Or where shall I flee from your presence? If I ascend up into heaven, you are there; if I make my bed in Sheol, behold, you are there; if I take the wings of the morning, and dwell in the uttermost parts of the sea, even there shall your hand lead me, and your right hand shall hold me.

In his book Brother Lawrence tells us how he accomplished the feat of consciously remaining in the presence of God all the time. It encouraged me as I read his book, because I realized if it were possible for him, it just might be possible for me and for you! I like to think of Brother Lawrence as I do a tennis pro. When you play with someone who is a lot better than you are, you play harder, you try harder, and subsequently you are pulled up to a higher level of performance. Spiritually, Brother Lawrence was on a very high level. In his book, he made this very thought provoking statement: "I no longer just believe, I see and experience."[11] As I read his book he tells over and over again how he was able to abide in God's presence all the time. He did it by repetition. He tells us how he kept on keeping on - doing it over and over and over. We all know that's how we improve any skill that is learned by repetition. In tennis, we do the same thing over and over and over again. Turn your side to the net! Don't forget! Don't hold that racket with a hammer grip! Practice, practice and practice until you get it and it becomes yours. Brother Lawrence's book is a practical spiritual application of how we, today, can live moment by moment in God's presence. He outlines some very important spiritual techniques that will help us to reach our goal if we will practice, practice, and practice.

In his book Brother Lawrence is already in the habit of abiding. He actually deals with how He maintained his relationship with God every minute of the day. But how did he get there? And even more important, how do we get there? What are the things that can block or hinder our way and keep it from happening? And what are the things that can help us in the process to make it happen?

First, let me point out something very important. Abiding in Christ moment by moment doesn't just happen. It didn't just happen with Brother Lawrence and it's not going to just happen with us. Brother Lawrence heart's desire was for God. And for this to happen in our lives our heart's desire must also be for God.

---

[11] The Practice of the Presence of God, p 71

Remember Psalms 42:1: *As the hart pants after the water brook, so pants my heart after thee, O God.* We must be panting for God. We must be hungry for Him. He must be our first Love. It's not going to happen to those who don't want it, who are not eagerly seeking and searching for it. (They don't have to be afraid it will happen)! But when we determine, set our wills that it be accomplished in our lives, it will, because God is always there, eagerly waiting for us to get to this point in our lives. Brother Lawrence tells us that "neither skill nor knowledge is needed to go to God. All that is necessary is a heart dedicated entirely and solely to Him out of a love for Him above all others."[12]

So let me reiterate: if we want to get there, we must first search our hearts and make sure our desire is for Him. We must yearn for Him, seek after Him, and want Him with all our heart. We must want Him more than anything in the world because we love Him so much.

---

12   The Practice of the Presence of God, p 18

Take Off Your Shoes

PART III:
Blocks that can keep it from happening

Take Off Your Shoes

DISOBEDIENCE

Can keep it from happening

For this is the love of God, that we keep his commandments. (1 John 5:3)

If you keep my commandments, you shall abide in my love, even as I have kept my Father's commandments and abide in his love. (John 15:10)

Jesus set down certain rules to guide us, to show us how we can abide always in Him. One day, one of His disciples asked, *"Lord, how is it that you will manifest yourself unto us and not unto the whole world"?* Jesus' reply was a clincher that holds the key for us to abide in Him always. He gave us a promise with a condition. This is what He said in John 14:23 and He repeats it three times, *"If a man loves me, He will keep my words and my Father will love him, and we will come unto him and make our abode with him."* So what is the condition? We must love Him enough to obey Him. And the promise? If we obey, He and His Father will love us and come make their home with us. So Jesus is telling us it doesn't just happen. There are conditions that we must meet. If we want it to happen, we have got to do something. He says we must love Him enough to keep His words. We must obey Him. Again in John 14:21 Jesus says, *"He that hath my commandments, and keeps them, he it is that loves me; and he that loves me shall be loved by my Father, and I will love him and will manifest (show) myself to him"* – will live with him!

I believe that we flip-flop in our relationship with Him in the exact proportion that we flip-flop in our obedience to His commands. Disobedience can dull our conscience, darken our soul and deadens our spiritual energies. We must be careful of disobedience even in little things. Obedience is the key to our abiding in Him. As we keep His commands – He dwells with us. That's a given.

It is of utmost importance that we get those commands off the page and into our lives. It makes sense, we've got to first know what they are, if we are going to obey them. We must not only study, understand, and memorize the scriptures, they must take root, must become the fiber of our being and until they do, they are not really ours. Just to know them is not enough - we've got to live them. Once, I was teaching a group of high school students, and my teenage son was present. I was telling them how important it is to know God's commandments and that He holds us responsible for what we know. My son just listened and never said a word. But the next Sunday when I awakened him to go to Sunday School, he told me he wasn't going. I asked him why (we went every Sunday). He replied: "Remember what you said the other night about being responsible for what we know? I already know enough!" But if we have determined to spend our lives in His presence, we have got to know what He commands and then obey. That's why studying God's word is so important. We must study and practice. We must practice and study. Jesus knew it wouldn't be easy. He didn't, however, make it an option. He didn't mean for us to try to keep His commandments - He meant for us to actually keep them. A few years ago I was driving into Baton Rouge and a huge billboard caught my attention. "LOVE YOUR ENEMIES - I MEAN IT! LOVE, GOD." Seeing that billboard took me off guard and made me realize how good I am at picking and choosing and rationalizing the commandments to fit my life. That's another big reason why I spend a lot of time flip-flopping in my relationship with God.

Once when my husband and I were visiting in France, we went to see the beautiful cathedral in Chartres. I'll never forget what our guide told us as he pointed out those magnificent stained glass windows and told us their story. He said that the Old Testament is the New Testament veiled, the New Testament is the Old Testament unveiled. I believe that what Jesus told His disciples in this 14th chapter of John (that obedience is the key to abiding in Him) is an unveiling in the New Testament of what God told Moses in the Old Testament. In Exodus 40:1-33 we find Moses erecting the tabernacle in the wilderness and following God's instructions to the letter. Eight times in this chapter it says that Moses followed God's instructions *as the Lord commanded him.* He obeyed! Now the exciting part is what happened after Moses obeyed everything God had commanded him to do. God filled the tabernacle with His presence. In fact, the presence of God was so mighty, so overwhelming, that Moses couldn't even enter in. *Then a cloud covered the tent of the congregation, and the glory of the Lord filled the tabernacle. And Moses was not able to enter into the tent of the congregation, because the cloud abode thereon, and the glory of the Lord filled the tabernacle. (Exodus 40:34-35)*

Stop for a minute and think of the mind boggling possibilities of our love and obedience to Him today. Did He not tell us that as Christians, our bodies are the temple of the living God? *Know you not that you are the temple of God and that the spirit of God dwells in you"? (1 Corinthians 3:16)* What the Shekinah glory was to the Tabernacle that Moses built, the Holy Spirit is to the temple which is the believer's body. So, as Moses obeyed God's commands, God filled the tabernacle with His Shekinah Glory. Today, as we obey God's commands, God fills us to overflowing with His Holy Spirit. There is also an incredible by-product of the Holy Spirit dwelling in us. We are given direction and guidance just as the Israelites in the Old Testament. *For the cloud of the Lord was upon the tabernacle by day, and fire was on it by night, in the sight of all the house of Israel, throughout all their journeys. (Exodus 40:38)*

Sin

Can keep it from happening

We know that whosoever is born of God sins not; but he that is begotten of good keeps himself, and that wicked one touches him not. (1 John 5:18)

I think we would all agree that disobedience is the number one block that keeps us from being aware of God's presence with us. Another word for disobedience is "sin." When we disobey, we sin. When we break God's commands, we sin. It's as simple as that. And as we know, sin has separated, and always will separate us from God. It all started in the Garden and it still happens today.

We cannot expect to abide with God and walk in sin at the same time. We fool ourselves if we think we can. I call it the Great Deception. Let me give you an example. I have this young friend who lives in another city, who was going through a really difficult divorce. She has children, and, in the midst of all the confusion, she invited her boyfriend to move in with her and the children. At the same time she was involved in a Bible Study which sometimes met in her home. She calls me frequently, and when she told me what was going on, I told her that it was not right for her boyfriend to be living with her, in fact, she was breaking one of God's commandments. She told me she thought that God would rather her live with this man and find out if they were compatible before she married him and made another mistake in marriage. She sincerely believed this was OK! I cannot find any scripture, old or new, that substantiates this reasoning. As a nation we are in deep trouble living under these kinds of delusions regarding sex and marriage. They are rampant! Recently, a friend told me that he did not think there was a thing wrong with two "old" people living together without the benefit of marriage. Then, he said, "I think it's OK for young people to live together without being married until they get ready to have a baby. Certainly you don't think that's wrong"? I told him that I certainly did think it was wrong and the Bible teaches us that it is wrong in 1 Corinthians 6:9-10. Furthermore, it doesn't matter what I think; it doesn't matter what you think; what matters is what God says! It is a delusion to think that God will bend the rules to accommodate what we think. Let me reiterate, we cannot walk with God, and walk in sin at the same time.

As Christians we do not deliberately sin, but when we do slip and sin, we must quickly confess and repent so that our relationship with God and our awareness of His presence will not be broken. *If we confess our sins, He is faithful and just to forgive us our sins, and cleanse us from all unrighteousness. (1 John 1:9)* So if we do sin, we must quickly make amends so that we can keep that relationship in good repair. And just for the record: there is no sin too big for God to forgive!

As Jesus told us in John 14, if we obey Him, He will come and live with us. So, as we live our lives out in His presence, what happens if we willingly disobey? Do you think it breaks the continuity of His presence with us? If so, it blows away that notion that many people have that He is always with us – sinning or not. I know from experience that when I am fully aware of God's presence in my life and I sin, it is like turning the lights off. I am the most miserable person alive when I am not aware of His presence with me.

Sin is an abomination in our lives. God hates sin and we should too. So why do we do it? I think one of our biggest problems is we don't really believe it when Jesus tells us we don't have to sin. Most of the Christians I know are programmed to sin. They not only sin, but they expect to sin, and expect to sin everyday. In my lifetime I have heard more than one minister tell us this from the pulpit – that sin in our lives is inevitable. In one sermon, the minister asked the congregation how many times they had sinned before they got to church that morning. This may be true before we give our lives to Jesus, but after we become Christians, we are God's children.

We live in His Kingdom and have the awesome privilege of asking Him for strength and power to keep us from sinning. My question is why would Jesus waste His breath telling us we can live in obedience to His commands, if it were not possible?

We all know that Jesus has set the standard very high, and we look at it and say there's no way we can do it. Love our enemy, no way! Do you really believe Jesus meant that we could obey His commands? I don't think He said it just to make us feel guilty and frustrated. He knew we couldn't do it in our own strength, and that's why He sent the Holy Spirit to help us in our weakness. Each morning we have to ask Him to give us His strength and His power to enable us to obey His commandments for that one day. We have to change our mindset. We have to EXPECT NOT TO SIN! Do you remember the man who was waiting for the water to stir at the pool near the sheep gate? The person who jumped in first was healed. This man had been there for forty years (imagine) and every time the water stirred, someone got in before he did. He had lost all expectation of being the first one in. When we lose our expectation, we lose the battle. BELIEVE YOU DON'T HAVE TO SIN! Jesus tells us in Mark 9:23, *"If you can believe, all things are possible to him that believes."* Believing something is possible is half the battle. When we believe, it connects us with God's power. It plugs us in!

One Thanksgiving, years ago, when our first five grandchildren were very small, I wanted to take a picture of them to put on our Christmas card. I enlisted their parents' help in the endeavor. As it turned out, taking pictures of those five kids was like trying to take a picture of five squirrels running around outside. It just seemed impossible. The parents gave up, but I was determined. I went into the den where the parents had gone to relax and asked them: "Is there anybody in this room who believes that taking this picture is possible"? One hand went up. "OK, come with me and the rest of you stay right here." You see, disbelief is like having a weight around your neck. My son, Paul, and I went outside, and believing it was possible, it happened!

So first, we have to believe it's possible not to sin and then expect not to sin if we want this 24/7 awareness of His presence with us. The second thing we have to do is to choose not to sin. The choice is ours whether we will sin or will not sin. It resides in our wills. We don't sin because we're sinners. We sin because we choose to. Remember, God is voting for us all the time - Satan is voting against us all the time - the way we vote carries the election. It's our choice! How will we choose? Will we or will we not? I remember a Sunday School teacher who likened our bad choices to going over a waterfall. There is a moment of decision, when we have to choose good over bad or bad over good. If our choice is bad over good, we go over that waterfall and say goodbye to our better self. I believe it is the same way with sin, except when we choose to sin and go over that waterfall, we say goodbye not to just our better self but to the awareness of our loving relationship with God.

Here is a sobering thought. If we are living, moving, and having our being in Him and are fully aware of His awesome presence, what happens when we do choose to sin? Do we ask Him to close His eyes or do we blindfold Him? Trust me on this one, He is right there watching us while we sin. (Remember the song, His Eye Is On The Sparrow and I know He watches me)? I recall a young couple in my Sunday School class. The husband had an affair. It was a terribly painful experience for his wife and for me as I watched her go through it. When he returned from his weekend of folly, he told me one of the hardest things for him was knowing how hurt I would be when I found out. Can you even begin to imagine how God must feel when we deliberately sin, fully aware that it not only breaks God's heart, but will also break that awareness of our relationship with Him? In 1 Chronicles 4:10 Jabez prayed, *"O Lord, keep me from evil, that it may not grieve me."* (I know in my life when I sin and I cause God pain, it is my greatest sorrow).

As with everything we practice in life, it becomes easier and easier as we practice. We must practice expecting not to sin, and practice choosing not to sin. As we do, it will become easier. Don't swallow that bait that you will sin, and you will sin every day. That is simply not true. Jesus would not have wasted His time telling us not to sin, if He didn't know it was possible.

Also, being accountable to a person, when we do sin will help us think twice before we make that bad choice to sin. I've often envied my Catholic friends who have to go to confession and speak out their sins to another human being. Although we can go straight to God and ask his forgiveness, I think it's an added incentive not to sin, when we know we will have to tell "someone with skin" about it.

The bottom line is this: we cannot tolerate sin and disobedience in our lives if we hope to make the awareness of God a reality in our lives. In Matthew 5:8 we are told that sin clouds the face of God. As Jesus preached the Sermon on the Mount, He told us, *"Blessed are the pure in heart; for they shall see God."* (Matthew 5:8) I've always thought of being pure as being without sin. That being sinless would make us pure. But did you know that we can be totally sinless and at the same time be as dry as a desert in our relationship with God? There is more to purity than sinlessness. If we keep sin out of our lives we shall see God. And as we see God we are changed into His image. *But we all, with unveiled face beholding as in a mirror the glory of the Lord, are changed into the same image from glory to glory, even as by the Spirit of the Lord.* (2nd Corinthians 3:18) So being pure affords us the opportunity to see, to behold God and as we do, we are changed into His image. "God Calling"[13] (June 2) puts it this way: *True it is today as it was in the days of Moses that no man can see my face and live. The self, the original man, shrivels up and dies, and upon the soul becomes stamped my image.*

---

13 God Calling by Two Listeners, Edited By A.J. Russell, p 115 Dodd, Mead and Company, New York, 1945

And how beautiful it is to see God in people. Recently I was selling my book, "Rainbows and Promises," at a boutique, and as the streams of people walked by, it was very interesting to watch them. In some of the people, you could see God in the lines of their face; in others, it was the way they spoke; in some it was the way they encouraged; in others it was their approachability. Their peace and joy were tangible. I like to think of these people as "burning bushes" that God shines through to reveal Himself.

Take Off Your Shoes

BEING DISHONEST
Can keep it from happening

One of the biggest problems that cause us to slip into sin is that we are simply not honest. We are not willing to call some things in our lives "sin" even though they are. We rationalize sin in order to justify it, so we can keep doing it. Have you ever had the wheels of your mind start turning and play out in detail a grievance against you? You start thinking about it and in some sort of weird way it gives you pleasure. Ever been there? Did you know that your thoughts can make you a rebellious child of God? When you need to forgive and you know it, you may be thinking: "But I have a right to feel this way! Just look what she did to me!"

We must be careful of what we think because we become what we think. I love what Brother Lawrence said about thinking: "Thinking spoils everything. Evil begins with our thoughts."[14] We all know that we can't stop evil thoughts from coming to us, just like we can't stop birds from flying over our heads. But just as we don't let those birds make a nest in our hair, likewise, we shush those evil thoughts away and don't let them make a nest in our mind. There are two scriptures that really help me with this problem. One is from Psalm 139:23-24: *Search me, O God, and know my heart; try me and know*

---
14   The Practice of the Presence of God, p.13

my thoughts; And see if there be any wicked way in me, and lead me in the way everlasting. Memorizing that verse and repeating it often, has made me more honest. It also connects me to His power and strength so that I am better able to resist evil. The other is from Philippians 4:8: *Finally, brethren, whatever things are true, whatever things are honest, whatever things are just, whatever things are pure, whatever things are lovely, whatever things are of good report; if there be any virtue, and if there be any praise, think on these things.* We can use this Scripture as a "check list" for our thoughts to make sure they are lined up with what God wants us to think.

BEING STUBBORN
Can keep it from happening

Another problem that can cause us to fall into the trap of sin is stubbornness. We just hang on, simply not wanting to give up a sin in our life that we know is there and we know it shouldn't be there. A good example is the woman that I met at a retreat years ago. She was very sick and asked one of the ministers to pray for her to get well. Before he prayed for her, he asked her if there was anything in her life that might block God's healing power. She confessed that she had a great and chronic grievance against a woman who had wronged her years ago and that she had never been able to forgive her. The minister said, "If you want to get well, you will have to forgive her first." Her reply: "I'd rather die!"

Are we guilty of doing the same thing? Do we harbor ill feelings and unforgiveness in our lives that could block blessings that God has for us? Not being able to forgive is probably the toughest sin we have to deal with. It's like cancer; if not removed, it keeps growing and eventually our lives are overwhelmed, smothered with hatred. (I have witnessed this happen in a young man I know, and it is frightening). Our enemy is not the person we can't forgive, our real enemy is hatred, caused by unforgiveness. Hatred lurks around the corner, just waiting to destroy us. When hatred takes root in our heart it not only separates us from God, it ultimately kills us spiritually and physically. Failing to forgive is like taking a dose of poison and waiting for the other person to die. It does more harm to the person in whom it is stored, than to the person upon whom it is poured. Our enemy Satan knows he's going to win the battle if he can just keep us from forgiving. Forgiveness leads to life and should be the lifestyle of a Christian. Forgiving seventy times seventy is not an old adage, but was spoken by Jesus when Peter asked Him, *"Lord, how often shall my brother sin against me, and I forgive him? Till seven time"? (Matthew 18:21) Jesus replied, "I say not unto thee until seven times; but, until seventy times seven." (Matthew 18:22)* And we as Christians should not expect forgiveness to be painless. Think of how much pain Jesus suffered in order that our sins could be forgiven. Ultimate forgiveness = Ultimate pain.

    Did you know that we can get hooked when we don't forgive? Every time we see that person that we can't forgive our button gets pushed. The adrenaline starts flowing through our veins. Do you know how you can tell when you have truly forgiven that person? They no longer have the capacity to push your button. You see them, and you can't even remember what the grievance was. When I was in graduate school there was a professor at the university that gave me a difficult time. In fact, she made my life miserable. The longer she harassed me, the deeper my dislike for her became. I carried this grievance around for years after I graduated. I didn't see her often, but when I did see her, those hostile feeling would surface and it was difficult for me to be civil. I had a hard time even speaking to her. I was convicted of this unforgiveness and God showed me it was a sin to harbor these bad feeling in my heart. I prayed mightily that God would forgive me and free me from this bondage. I never thought anymore about it until a few years later when a friend invited me to play in her tennis league. When I arrived at the tennis club, much to my surprise, the now retired professor was there. She was not only in the league; she was to be my partner for the day. What was even more surprising was that my adrenaline did not rise up, and there were absolutely no hostile feelings that surfaced. In fact, I had a hard time remembering why I had been so offended by her. I believe that God orchestrated that meeting to let me know that when I was weak and unforgiving, all I had to do was to ask Him to forgive me and deliver me from that unforgiveness. And He did the rest. To forgive is to set the prisoner free, only to discover that the prisoner is me.

Take Off Your Shoes

Hurry and Busyness

Can keep it from happening

We must carefully watch for common everyday things that contribute to blocking our awareness of God's presence with us. One of those things is haste and another is busyness. I can identify with Emily Dickinson who said, "To live is so startling, it leaves little time for anything else." I make a list a mile long in the morning and then I tell myself, "Now do it." And no matter how hard I try, I usually end up frustrated, and sometimes by the end of the day I am a basket case. I set goals too high, and then I become stressed as I rush to accomplish them. In my haste to attain those goals, I'm the loser. Haste becomes like an old-fashioned ink blotter that soaks up all our peace, contentment, and joy and can even blot out the awareness of God's presence with us.

Brother Lawrence said we must do everything with great care, avoiding impetuous actions which are evidence of a disordered spirit. God wants us to work gently, calmly, humbly and lovingly without giving way to anxiety or problems. (My question is, how will I get it all done if I follow Brother Lawrence's advice?) We must ask God to remove whatever it is that does not lead to Him. I also pray for God to give me the enthusiasm for what He wants me to do. That enthusiasm (God in us) energizes me to do those things that He wants me to do. So, if I am not enthusiastic about doing something, then I just don't do it. This works for me and has helped eliminate a lot of stress in my life.

Remember what Jesus told Martha in Luke 10:41, when she complained about Mary sitting at Jesus' feet while she was busy doing all the work? *"Martha, Martha, you are worried and upset about many things, but only one thing is needed. Mary has chosen what is better and it will not be taken away from her."* He is much more interested in what we "are" than in what we "do." We all know that the work must be done, but we should keep it in balance. We must spend as much time as possible "sitting at Jesus feet". *"But seek ye first the Kingdom of God, and his righteousness, and all these things shall be added unto you."* (Matthew 6:33)

Distractions
Can keep it from happening

Distractions can trip us up. We truly live in a world of mass distractions, and we don't have to look for them. They are everywhere. I was sitting in the airport not long ago, and, as I sat there, the TV was going overhead and many of the people around me were talking on their cell phones. (I get so tired of hearing one-sided conversations. I often wonder what we did before cell phones). Then there are those things that pop up without provocation to distract us. Years ago my two daughters-in-law were having lunch with their four toddlers. The children were whooping, hollering and into everything. After the girls finished eating one looked at the other and asked, "Did we eat"? Distractions not only cloud our relationship with God, they can make us forget that we ever had one.

We can't become so involved in the distractions of the world that our awareness of God becomes choked out. Remember the parable of the sower in Matthew 13? One of the places he planted seeds was among thorns, and the thorns choked the seedlings out. Jesus likened those thorns to the cares and the distractions of the world, which can also do the same thing to our relationship with Him.

Take Off Your Shoes

Fear

Can keep it from happening

Have I not commanded you? Be strong and courageous. Do not be terrified; do not be discouraged, for the Lord your God is with you wherever you go. (Joshua 1:9 NIV)

Another thing that blocks our relationship with God is fear, fear of what that relationship will cost us, fear that we are not good enough to be close to God. Discouragement is one of the tools that Satan uses to keep us from having a close relationship with God. He does everything to discourage us and destroy our relationship because he doesn't want us to have one. Another fear is of God Himself. In the Scriptures He calmed people who were afraid of Him. *And when the disciples saw him walking on the sea, they were troubled, saying, It is a ghost; and they cried out for fear. But straightway Jesus spoke unto them, saying, "Be of good cheer, it is I; be not afraid." (Matthew 14:26-27)*

Jesus didn't say there would not be things to fear. He simply told us not to be afraid because He would be with us and that He would give us His peace. He didn't say that He would still the storm that is raging around us, but that He would still the storm within us.

For God has not given us the spirit of fear, but of power, and of love, and of a sound mind. (2 Timothy 1:7)

Submit yourself, therefore, to God. Resist the devil, and he will flee from you. (James 4:7)

If we want this awesome awareness of God's presence with us, we must be diligent and watchful for any of these "blocks" that can trip us and cause us to fall into sin. Sin committed, unacknowledged, and not repented of is the most common barrier to our continual fellowship with God and communion with Him. The fight against sin is no half-hearted business. It means a declaration of war and war to the end! Our enemy, Satan, wants nothing more than for us to disobey Father God and interrupt our relationship with Him. But every battle can be won through our faith in God and His strength. Brother Lawrence said he sinned only when he strayed from God's presence or when he forgot to ask Him for help.

Remember what God told Abraham in Genesis 17:1, *"I am the almighty God; walk before me and be ye perfect."*

*PART IV:
Helps to make
it happen*

I asked the almond tree, Sister, speak to me of God and the almond tree blossomed.
The glory of God is a human being fully alive. [15]

N. Kazantzakis

---

15   Attributed to N. Kazantzakis, 20th Century

There are times when the holiness of God breaks through to the ordinary. Some people refer to these times as "thin places" in their lives, others call them "altars." I call them "burning bushes." I believe they are all around us, separated only by a very thin veil caused by our disobedience and sin. God is eager to reveal Himself to us and hopefully these "helps" will make us more cognizant of His presence with us, more aware of the "burning bushes" all around us. I want my life laced with these "thin places," not just as I approach death, but every day of my life.

I want to preface this section of "Take Off Your Shoes" with something of an apology. In these "helps" I have used very personal experiences that I have had with God. Frank Laubach in his book "Letters to a Modern Mystic" [16] said it this way, "In defense of my opening my soul and laying it bare to the public gaze in this fashion, I may say that it seems to me that we really seldom do anybody much good excepting as we share the deepest experiences of our souls in this way. And I hunger. O how I hunger! For others to tell me their soul adventures."

---

[16] Letters by a Modern Mystic by Frank C. Laubach, pp 12,13 Fleming H. Revell Company, Westwood, NJ

Take Off Your Shoes

QUIET TIMES

Help to make it happen

Be still and know that I am God. (Psalm 46:10)
For thus saith the Lord God, the Holy One of Israel: In returning and rest shall you be saved; in quietness and in confidence shall be your strength. (Isaiah 30:15)
Delight yourself also in the Lord, and He shall give you the desires of your heart. (Psalm 37)

We must get in the habit of stopping each day to spend a quiet, uninterrupted time with God. As we are told in 1st Thessalonians 4:11: *We must study to be quiet.* God told us that if we are to know Him, we must be still. So it is our responsibility to avail ourselves to this stillness, this quietness, free from all the distractions around us so that we can talk to Him and He can talk to us, so that we can get to know Him better and become aware of His presence always. Being still and quiet calms us down and avails us to God's presence so that we can experience Him. D.L. Moody said that we as Christians "talk cream and live skimmed milk."[17] If we want that richness of soul, the fullness of God's presence in our lives, we will find it in the quiet time that we set apart daily to spend with Him.

This quiet time is best done early in the day and, if possible,

---
17 Quotation attributed to evangelist D.L. Moody

in a special place where we meet God. I have my quiet time early in the morning. I sit in my den where I can look outside and see His handiwork: the trees, the flowers, the birds, and all His little creatures running around. I especially love to see redbirds because they always remind me that God is right there with me. Going to God early prepares us for the rest of the day and affords us the opportunity to invite Him to be an integral part of our lives all day long. During this time we can also ask Him for His guidance and ask Him to show us what he wants us to do.

It is imperative that we have this quiet time every single day. I believe that the gathering of the manna in the Old Testament is symbolic of our quiet time with God. Remember, the manna had to be collected every day and it was sufficient to sustain them for that one day only. If they gathered enough for two days, the second day's portion would spoil. (Only on Friday, the day before the Sabbath, could they collect it for two days). So, just as the Israelites had to collect their manna everyday, we also have to collect our manna everyday, spending quiet time with God. And just as the Israelites couldn't collect their manna for two days, neither can we. We can't have a quiet time with God one day and expect it to last two days. We have to form the habit of spending time with him every single day and asking Him to *"Give us this day our daily bread." (Matthew 6:11)*

Theodore Roosevelt said it this way: "You may worship God anywhere at any time, but the truth is that you will not do so unless you have first learned to worship Him somewhere in some special place at some particular time."[18] Certainly this is true of our quiet time with God. And forming the habit of spending time with God every single day is not easy. With a thousand things yelling for our attention, I'm sure we would all agree it is very difficult. But it's not impossible, and it is probably the most important thing we ever accomplish in our lives. The secret of making the awareness of God real in our lives is discovered when we set apart this specific period of time each day to spend with Him. If we don't set it apart like Roosevelt said, we won't do it. Our quiet time must have a fixed place, somewhere free from distractions and where we feel comfortable. One of the reasons a fixed place is important is because sometimes God will surprise us and get there first. So with a special time and a fixed place, the battle is won. And we must be diligent. It's much easier if we do it regularly. I confess that I fail over and over again to keep that relationship unbroken by not being diligent and by being careless with my quiet time. Remember, when we grow careless in our technique of approach to God, we grow less sensitive to His presence.

Some things are important for my quiet time. One is my Bible. I also have favorite devotion books. Some of my very favorites are "God Calling",[19] "My Utmost for His Highest"[20] and "31 Days of Praise"[21]. I especially like "God Calling" because it is written as if God Himself is speaking. I have read it for many years and without fail, it ministers to me.

---

18 Quotation attributed to Theodore Roosevelt
19 God Calling
20 My Utmost for His Highest by Oswald Chambers Dodd, Mead and Company, New York, 1966
21 31 Days of Praise

Now what do we do in our quiet time with God? A good way to start is by telling Him how much we love Him. We are talking to the same God who told us that the most important commandment for us to keep is, *"Love the Lord your God with all your heart, and with all your soul, and with all your mind." (Matthew 22:37).*

Second, thanksgiving and praise play a big part in our quiet time because they usher us into His presence. Psalm 100:1, 2, 4 reads:

Make a joyful noise unto the Lord, all ye lands.

Serve the Lord with gladness; come before his presence with singing.

Enter into his gates with thanksgiving, and into his courts with praise.

Also, we are told in Psalm 22:3 that *God inhabits the praises of His people.*

We can invite Him to be with us all day long and thank Him for the awesome privilege of allowing us to live in His shadow. As it is written in Psalm 91:1: *He who dwells in the secret place of the Most High shall abide under the shadow of the Almighty.* We can ask Him to be an integral part of every circumstance, to help us make decisions and to give us direction about what we should do and where we should go. I often pray, "Lord, if you don't go with me, I'm not going either." I love and quote Proverbs 3:5 many times during the day, *Trust in the Lord with all your heart, and lean not on your own understanding. In all your ways acknowledge Him, and He shall direct your paths.* We can speak to Him about our problems and concerns, and intercede for those whom we carry in our heart. We can actually talk to Him about anything that is on our heart and mind.

But we can't do all the talking. We have to save some of our quiet time to give God a chance to talk to us. We must be in the mental and spiritual attitude of the child, Samuel, when he said, *"Speak Lord, for your servant is listening." (1 Samuel 3:10)* Remember Samuel was sleeping in one room and Eli in another room. Samuel heard a voice. He arose, thinking it was Eli. He went into his room and asked him what he said. Eli told him he had not spoken, so Samuel went back to bed, only to hear the voice again. This happened three times. Eli told Samuel that it was the Lord speaking to him and to say when he heard it again, *"Speak Lord, for your servant is listening."*

So we must expect God to talk to us and we must be listening. How does He speak to us during these quiet times? He speaks to our hearts, our spirits, and even our minds. When we are quiet before Him, He will sometimes pour thoughts and ideas into our mind.

Do you ever wonder if what you perceived to be from God was really from Him? One time this man went to his minister because he thought that God had spoken to him and told him to do something, but he wasn't sure it was God. The minister listened and when the man told him what he thought God wanted him to do, the minister said, "Go for it man, the devil doesn't call people to do that kind of work!" This is where our knowledge of Scripture comes in handy, because God will never ask us to do anything that is contradictory to what He has already told us in the Scriptures. Psalm 119:105 tells us: *Thy word is a lamp unto my feet, and a light unto my path.*

So it is very important that we make reading the Bible a part of our quiet time. It gives God a chance to speak to us clear and simple. After all, the Bible is the instruction book that God gave us to follow. When I was a teenager and young adult I habitually read a chapter of my Bible every night before I went to bed. I have to confess that sometimes my eyes read those words without my mind having a clue of what my eyes were reading. But if we read until we learn something, it helps our mind focus on what our eyes are reading.

Another very important thing that happens during our quiet time is that God fills us up with Himself. There are some people who expect very little of God. The sum of their Christian life is "to agree on some basic beliefs" and that's it. They expect only an eye-dropper full of God. But the Scriptures tell us that we are to live in the Fullness of God's presence – filled to the brim, pressed down and running over. One time when I was visiting my son in Natchez, I went to bed around 10 p.m. At that time my grandson was 8 years old, and I could hear him running around the house, into everything, just full of energy. At one point, he came to my door and knocked, and when he came in, I said, "Peyton, isn't it your bedtime? Shouldn't you be in bed"? His reply was, "Gran, I can't go to bed, my tank is full!"

And this is what we want in our relationship with God. We want our tanks to be overflowing with Him. But for this to happen we must make ourselves available for Him to fill us up. It's like taking our car to the gas station. That doesn't just happen; we have to take the car to the station to get it filled up. Likewise, each day in our quiet time, we take ourselves into God's presence and ask Him to fill us up with Himself. So full that our eyes will see as He sees, our ears will hear as He hears, our hearts will love as He loves, our mouths will speak as He speaks, (words of life, instead of death, good instead of evil), our wills will obey as He obeys, and our minds will have the understanding of the mind of Christ.

As we spend this quiet time with Him, seeking His face, beholding His Glory, we are changed into His image. (2nd Corinthians 3:18) We do not change ourselves. God changes us. We do not make ourselves humble, patient, loving, and strong. We live with God and He does that for us.

Take Off Your Shoes

BEHOLDING

Helps to make it happen

O Zion, that brings good tidings, get thee up into the high mountain! O Jerusalem, that brings good tidings, lift up thy voice with strength; lift it up, be not afraid; say unto the cities of Judah, behold your God! (Isaiah 40:9)

He has made everything beautiful in its time and has set eternity in our heart. (Ecclesiastes 3:11)

But blessed are your eyes, for they see; and your ears, for they hear. (Matthew 13:16)

In John 17:24, Jesus prayed this prayer for us. *"Father, I will that they also, whom you have given me, be with me, where I am, that they may behold my glory, which thou hast given me."* He prayed this prayer for us, you and me, for right now, here on earth. He wants us to behold His glory. He prayed to Father God, to make this happen. So, how do we get to where He is and be with Him so that we might see His glory?

Do you remember what Jesus told Nicodemus in John 3:3? He said, *"Verily, verily, I say unto you, except a man be born again, he cannot see the kingdom of God."* When we are born spiritually, He gives us spiritual eyes to see Him, spiritual ears to hear Him and a spiritual sense of feel that we might experience Him. He actually sends His Holy Spirit to dwell within us. Remember what we are told in 2 Corinthians 6:16: *For you are the temple of the living God; as God has said, I will dwell in them, and walk in them; and I will be their God and they shall be my people.* So He has already equipped us to not only be with Him where He is (He is as close as the air we breathe), but has given us eyes to behold His glory. I think this is what Brother Lawrence meant when he said, "I no longer just believe, I see and experience."[22]

So we want to see and experience the Kingdom of God. Remember, Jesus told us in the Sermon on the Mount, *"Blessed are the pure in heart; for they shall see God."* (Matthew 5:8) So if we are to behold Him we must keep our hearts pure and let no sin cloud our view. Once, years ago, in our young people's Bible Class, we likened sin in our lives to the soot that is generated by an old fashioned oil lamp. As you burn the lamp, the soot collects on the globe and turns it black. If not cleaned, that soot will eventually block the light from shining forth. Every day, that globe must be cleaned and the soot removed. Likewise, sin does the same thing to our hearts and keeps our spiritual eyes from seeing God. Every day, we must guard our hearts against being clouded by sin.

I love the little song that goes like this: *"Open our eyes Lord, we want to see Jesus, to reach out and touch Him, and tell Him we love Him. Open our ears Lord, and help us to listen, Open our eyes Lord, we want to see Jesus."*[23] This is a prayer we sing, asking God to open our eyes so that we might behold Him.

One summer my son and I went to the beach. I get so excited

---
22   The Practice of the Presence of God, p 71
23   Open Our Eyes by Robert Cull   Maranatha! Music, 1976

about going because I can really see and hear and feel the presence of God so mightily. When I'm there, I'm totally surrounded by His handiwork, and they are constant reminders that He is right there with me. When the sun comes up each morning, I begin the day awe struck by its incredible beauty. Then comes evening, and the sunset (as if the sunrise wasn't enough), with a glorious display of His artistic ability. Then comes night, with the light of the moon shimmering on the water and the stars decorating the sky with little twinkles of light. It's awesome! And the waves are an ever- present reminder that He is right there with me. As they roll onto the beach, over and over and over, you can almost hear Him saying, "I'm here, I'm here, I'm right here with you."

According to J.R.R. Tolkien in his book, *The Silmarillion*,[24] the reason people are drawn to the beach is because they can hear in the waves, the echo of the music that was playing when God created the earth. I was talking to my son about this, and he said to me, "I just don't see it Mother." I told him to go for a walk on the beach and ask God to open his eyes so he could see Him. (One of my very favorite stories in the Old Testament comes from 2 Kings 6:14-17. Elisha and his man servant were surrounded by the enemy and his servant was very frightened. Elisha prayed and asked God to open the eyes of his servant. And the Lord opened the eyes of the young man and he saw that the mountain was full of God's horses and chariots of fire all around them.) Well, it was like that with my son. He said he was going to pray for God to open his eyes while he was on his walk and when he got back, he burst into

---

24 The Silmarillion by J.R.R. Tolkien p.19 Houghton Mifflin Company, Boston, MA, 1977

the beach house and said, "Mama, He's everywhere!!"

In 1984, when I was going through a really trying time with one of the children, I happened to be at the beach and I arose really early to go for a walk. God gave me this poem, which actually fits into the tune of a song called, "My Last Farewell." I named it "Light and Glory" and it goes like this:

I see the tide, the ever moving water
I hear the roar and splash of power and might
The rising sun reflects your light and glory
And you are so beautiful, more beautiful my father,
Than any spoken word could ever say.
The white winged sea gulls fly and soar in splendor
Against a sky that reaches to the sea
The rising sun reflects your light and glory
And you are so beautiful, more beautiful my father,
Than any spoken word could ever say
The wonders of almighty God creator
Are in full view for everyone to see
The rising sun reflects your light and glory
And you are so beautiful, more beautiful my father,
Than any spoken word could ever say.
For you are beautiful, and I have learned to love you
More dearly as I spend these days with you.

One summer, my sister Bonnie, came to visit us at the beach. She had recently had a knee replacement, and one afternoon she was resting. It was getting close to sunset and I wanted her to see it. I didn't want to disturb her, but I could tell the sunset was going to be incredible. I went to her door and knocked. I said,

"Bonnie, get up and come see the sunset. And hurry, because it's about to set." (You don't tell a person who has recently had a knee replacement to hurry). Anyway, she finally got out on the porch and I can truly tell you it was the most beautiful sunset I've ever seen! As we stood, surrounded by His glory, I said to her, "Oh, Bonnie, God did this just for you!" One month later, Hurricane Katrina hit. Our beach house was totally obliterated - not one thing left! I was heartbroken, but with New Orleans and the Mississippi Coast so devastated, I tried not to lament over my loss. But God knew I was suffering. One day, without provocation, He said to me, "Anne, do you remember that beautiful sunset last month when Bonnie was at the beach house"? "Yes, Father, I remember, how could I forget"? "You told Bonnie that I did it just for her, but I did it for you!" *Blessed are they that mourn; for they shall be comforted. (Matthew 5:4).*

Remember, when Peter was walking on the water to get to where Jesus was; as long as he kept his eyes on Jesus, he did not sink.

How many million stars must shine
That only God can see,
Yet in His heaven His hand has hung
Ten million stars for me.[25]

Oh Lord, how incomprehensible art thou in thy thoughts, how profound in thy design and how powerful in all thy actions.[26]

Prayer. *Oh Lord, remove the scales from our eyes, as You did for Elijah's manservant, so that we can see You at work and not miss beholding Your glory.*

---
25 Practicing the Presence, p 105
26 The Practice of the Presence of God p 86

Take Off Your Shoes

REACHING OUT

Helps to make it happen

"*Compassion is not a command, it is a gift.*"[27]

Then shall the King say unto them on his right hand, Come, ye blessed of my Father, inherit the kingdom prepared for you from the foundation of the world;

For I was hungry, and you gave me food; I was thirsty, and you gave me drink; I was a stranger, and you took me in;

Naked, and you clothed me; I was sick, and you visited Me; I was in prison and you came unto me."

Then shall the righteous answer him saying, "Lord, when saw we you hungry, and fed you? Or thirsty, and gave you drink?

When saw we you a stranger, and took you in? Or naked, and clothed you?

Or when saw we you sick, or in prison, and came unto you"?

And the King shall answer and say unto them, Verily I say unto you, Inasmuch as you have done it unto one of the least of these my brethren, you have done it unto me. (Matthew 25:34-40)

One of easiest ways to be with Jesus and behold His glory is

---

[27] Unknown author

found right here in this Scripture. Let's stop and think about what Jesus just said in these verses. When we do it unto one of the least of these, we do it unto Him. That statement is staggering to me. As we reach out to help others in need, we are actually reaching out to Jesus Himself. Is not that mind-boggling?

Years ago, I took a course in our Wednesday Bible Class called "Experiencing God." Henry Blackaby, one of the authors, made a statement that stuck indelibly in my mind: "Look around and see where God is working and join Him."[28] I've tried to keep my eyes open to see where He is working, because I don't want to miss any chance of beholding His glory. When I first met Mack McCarter at Community Renewal International, I told him what Blackaby had said, and that I wanted to work with him at CRI, because I felt like God was at work there. (God is at work in many, many places, but this is the place where He lead me). One of the things that intrigued me about Community Renewal was the Friendship House in the very heart of Cedar Grove, a very poor and underprivileged neighborhood with an extremely high crime rate.

For many years I drove through Cedar Grove to get to my home. I saw the people as I passed by and my heart broke to think of them. I often prayed for them and thought how wonderful it would be if there was some way I could reach out to them. Community Renewal afforded the opportunity to actually span that great chasm between them and me. It opened the door for me to enter their world and get to know and love them.

My first job in Cedar Grove was sponsored by Community

---

28 Experiencing God by Henry T. Blackaby, Richard Blackaby, and Claude V. King Crossbooks, Indianapolis, Ind. 2007

Renewal, and it was called the "Sister School." A friend, Sari Joubert, (whose idea it was) and I worked for six months with thirteen young black girls and their mothers or sponsors. Every Saturday morning from eight to one o'clock we met with them at St. Catherine's activity building. We had a Bible Class, a class about how to dress properly, a class on personal hygiene, and a class on spending money wisely (since they didn't have any money, we actually gave them a little money, so they could experiment). Someone came in and talked to them about the dangers of drugs. Every week we talked to them about their dreams and aspirations, and that it was imperative for them to abstain from sex until they were married if their dreams were to be realized. At noon, one of the service clubs from the high schools brought lunch, and we taught the girls in the Sister School how to set the table. As we ate with them, we taught them proper table manners.

We did this for six months and on the very last day we had a special ceremony, a very meaningful experience where each mother was to make a mask for her daughter. Each girl had a mat, plaster of paris, and a pan of water to wet it. The lady who was to direct it was there. As the girls and their mothers began going into the next room to start the ceremony, one of the mothers and her daughter came up to me and said, "Miss Anne, Victoria wants you to do her mask". I said to the mother whose name was Vicky: "Oh, no Vicky, I can't do it, you have to do it yourself. You see, it's a ceremony for mothers and daughters." I remember that Vicky had a couple of front teeth missing, but when she said, "But Mrs. Anne, she loves you," I realized in that moment, I was looking into the face of God. I was beholding His glory. And just as sure as I am writing this today, He was telling me, "I love you." *Inasmuch as you have done it unto one of the least of these my brethren, you have done it unto me. (Matthew 25:40)*

My tears helped moisten the plaster of paris as I made Victoria's mask. I thought I had gone into Cedar Grove to reach out to them, to try to help them, and to love them. And it all boomeranged when God spoke to me and said, "I love you." Psalm 16:11 reads: *In his presence is the fullness of joy.* I cried all afternoon and into the night. I actually woke up a couple of times in the night and was still crying. I knew what Pascal meant when he said: "Oh, just Father, the world has not known you, but I know you. Joy, Joy, Joy! Tears of Joy!"[29]

We are told in Proverbs 19:17- NRS: *Whosoever is kind to the poor lends to the Lord, and will be repaid in full.* I believe the statement "they shall be repaid in full" means simply this: they shall be repaid by beholding the glory of God, by experiencing the overwhelming joy of seeing the Face of God.

Show me Your face Lord, Show me Your face. Then gird up my legs that I might stand in this holy place. [30]

---

29 Blaise Pascal
30 Song by Juanita Bynum

LISTENING

Helps to make it happen

Do you believe that God speaks to you? I do. After I wrote "Rainbows and Promises," I was interviewed by a young man from the local newspaper. One of the first questions he asked me was, "Why did you write this book"? My reply was "Because God asked me to." Complete silence, a void, a quizzical look. I had the uncomfortable feeling that he was waiting for me to say, "Just kidding!"

But God does speak to me, and it makes me uncomfortable when I have to apologize for it. Some people ask how I know He speaks to me, and I am quick to tell them that it's not with my physical ears that I hear Him (except when He speaks to me through other people). Mostly I hear Him speak to me with my spiritual ears, the ears I received when I was born spiritually and became His child. My spiritual ears give me the capacity to hear Father God and to communicate with Him. Actually, He speaks, and to tell the honest truth, lots of times I just simply don't listen because I don't want to obey.

Here's an example: one Sunday Morning my husband and I were at church, sitting in the balcony, where we always sit. As the service was coming to a close, God spoke to me and said: "I want you to go over and speak to that man." "That man" was someone sitting alone in the balcony. Immediately, my response was, "But, I don't know him. I don't even know his name and it would be so embarrassing to go over there and talk to him." So, I sat there, feeling like a disobedient child, very uncomfortable. As we began to sing the closing hymn, I leaned over to my husband and asked: "After church would you go over and speak to that man (pointing him out) with me"? He didn't say, "Why"? or "What are you talking about"? All he said was, "Sure." After the benediction, we went over to this man and introduced ourselves. I said, "We're so glad you're here!" Before I could say another word he said, "Thank you for coming over to speak to me. You see, I have never given my life to Christ. Can you tell me what to do"? I literally took him by the hand and said "Let's go downstairs and talk to our minister." The next Sunday he was baptized.

Dave had a doctorate in horticulture which he never mentioned. He was a very humble man, and, when asked what he did for a living, he simply said, "I'm a farmer." Among the crops he harvested were the most luscious peaches imaginable (the kind you have to hold your head over the sink to eat, because they are so juicy).

A couple of years after he became a Christian, as he was working on his farm riding a tractor, he went under a tree and a limb crashed down on him. He was killed. God is "all knowing" (omniscient). He can see into the future. He knows what's going to happen. So when He speaks to us, we just need to obey, even if we don't know everything that He knows. (That's what trust is).

At Dave's funeral, the minister said that Dave was a Christian and a woman who was there led him to Christ. I've always heard that the people you help lead to Christ will be your neighbors in heaven. The first thing I thought of when the minister said that was, "Hallelujah! I'll have those wonderful peaches in heaven!"

In one of her courses, Beth Moore told this heart wrenching story of God speaking to her in an airport. One day, as she sat waiting for her flight, she noticed a man with long mangled hair sitting near by. God spoke to her and asked her to go over and witness to him. She said she was not comfortable doing that and so she just sat there. God spoke to her again, this time asking her to go over and comb his hair. She immediately told God she would witness to him. Too late! She walked over to the man and asked, "Would you like for me to comb your hair"? He said "Yes, I wish you would." He then began crying and explained to her that he had been in an accident and had broken both his arms. In his rush to catch the plane, the hospital attendants had not had time to brush his hair and with both arms broken he couldn't raise his arms to do it himself. He told her he was on his way home and hadn't seen his wife for six months.

When God asks us to do something and we refuse, He will find someone else to do it. But the problem is that when we do refuse, we miss His blessing and miss beholding His Glory. One thing about obedience is this: all we have to do is to obey and then God does the rest. We just wait to see what happens.

When God speaks to us, it is not always to ask us to do something for him. Sometimes He just wants to talk to us. A few years ago, I noticed a much neglected flower bed in front of the friendship house in Cedar Grove where I taught a Bible Class. It was so pathetic that it made me sad as I walked by it, and I'm sure it made the students feel the same way. So I decided I would plant flowers. I asked one of the students to help me clean it out, dig up the hard, crusty dirt and put in some soft top soil so the flowers would have a chance to grow. I then went to the nursery and got some yellow and blue pansies. I'll never forget the day I planted them – it was the day that God spoke to me. It was a perfect Indian summer afternoon. As soon as I began planting the flowers, a school bus drove up and two little boys bolted out. One ran over to me. Out of breath he said, "Oh, can I help you"? "Sure," I said. "But go in first and tell them you're here and ask if it's OK." He was back in a flash and knelt down right beside me, planting the pansies. After a while, in the stillness of the afternoon, I heard that little 6-year-old boy say to me, "Thank you for doing this." Does God speak to us? You bet He does! And you'll know it when He does - without a shadow of a doubt.

PRAYING

Helps to make it happen

Pray without ceasing. (1 Thessalonians 5:17)
I urge, then, first of all, that requests, prayers, intercession and thanksgiving be made for everyone – for kings and all those in authority, that we may live peaceful and quiet lives in all godliness and holiness. (1 Timothy 2:1-2 NIV 1984)

What things do we do without ceasing? We breathe. Our hearts beat. Both have disastrous results if stopped. In this scripture we are instructed to pray without ceasing. That means we are to pray all the time and talk to God about everything. Praying without ceasing reminds us that we are never alone as we travel through life.

One way we can make this happen in our lives is to get in the habit of praying for everyone we meet, whether it's in the grocery store, on an airplane, driving the car, or in a restaurant. I heard about a woman who did this very thing. One day she and her small son were going to McDonald's for lunch. There was a wreck on the way, and as was her custom, she started praying for those involved. She said to her son, "Why don't you pray too"? From the back seat she heard him say "Dear God, please don't let that wreck keep us from getting into McDonalds."

Nothing helps us love someone as much as praying for them. We must practice praying for everyone around us, wherever we are. Think about the possibilities of this. If you pray without ceasing, you can't be thinking mean thoughts, you can't be worrying. I'll never forget one time I went to my doctor because I was having trouble sleeping at night. He asked me what I did when I couldn't sleep. I told him that mostly I would pray. "Pray"? he said. "That's the worst thing you could possibly do. It just brings all your problems to mind." But contrary to what the doctor said, we are instructed to pray without ceasing.

Brother Lawrence said that prayer consisted totally and simply of being in God's presence – when he wasn't in prayer he felt practically the same way as when he was. Like the little girl who said, "I think about God even when I'm not praying." Brother Lawrence remained near to God. He praised and blessed Him with all his strength, and because of this his life was full of continual joy.

Praying for other people wherever you go is very time consuming because it gets you involved. If you don't want to get involved, don't pray! This truth came home to me a few years ago. I had been out of town and was returning home. As I boarded the airplane I mapped out my agenda. I was scheduled to teach a lesson on prayer the next day and the time on the plane was my only chance to study. I had my Bible, a couple of study books, "What Happens When Women Pray"[31] and "All Things are Possible Through Prayer."[32] As soon as I found my seat, I got out my books, pens, and paper to start studying. As is my habit, I prayed before I started, not only that God would

---

31   What Happens When Women Pray by Evelyn Christenson   Chariot Victor Publishing, Peabody, MA
32   All Things are Possible Through Prayer by Charles Allen   Fleming H. Revell Company, Westwood, New Jersey, 1958

guide me in my study but also a prayer for the people on the plane.

When I finished praying, I looked up and I saw the flight attendant coming down the aisle with a precious little girl, probably five or six years old. She was decked out in her Sunday best. She wore a beautiful white lacy dress, lace trimmed socks, white Mary Janes, and to top it off, a white hat on her head. She was all smiles. Her seat was across the aisle from mine, but one row up. I could observe everything that followed. She settled in her seat and from all outward appearances, was just fine traveling alone. She seemed very grown-up for her age. That lasted until the door of the plane closed with a bang and that's when the trouble began. She started crying, loud enough for the flight attendant to hear from the front of the plane. The flight attendant came immediately and sat down next to her and started talking to her. It didn't work, she cried even harder! Another flight attendant came to help. Nothing they could do or say stopped her cries. They became louder and louder. Her grown-up resolve was completely gone and she was blatantly afraid.

Now remember the lady across the aisle and one row back? All this time I was praying for the little girl instead of studying. All of a sudden God whispers in my ear, "Go sit by her." "Me, Lord, Me? You know this is absolutely my only chance for preparing the lesson I've got to teach tomorrow." And yet I heard the crying from across the aisle. "OK, I'll do it. I couldn't study with her screaming anyway." I asked the very distraught flight attendant if I could sit with her and try my luck to calm her. In desperation she said, "Please do!"

The little girl was seated next to the window and the plane was out on the tarmac, ready to take off. I told her what was about to happen and how much fun it was going to be. Look out the window, and you'll see it all yourself. We're going to go really fast, and then we will soar into the sky. This distracted her, and she calmed down a little. As the plane started down the runway she grabbed my hand. By the time we were in the sky she had stopped crying and seemed excited about the whole thing. For the rest of the trip, I sat next to her, holding her hand, talking to her and answering a barrage of questions. She was especially fascinated by the incredibly beautiful cumulus clouds that looked exactly like great big fluffy cotton candy. I told her how God had created those clouds just for her to enjoy while she was flying.

When the flight attendant came to see about her, she was happy again. They said to me, "Thank you so much! Is there anything we can do for you? Would you like a drink on the house? Anything"? "No," I said, "Just pray that I will have a lesson tomorrow." Even as I spoke, I knew He had already prepared the lesson for me. Get in the habit of praying for people wherever you go - on planes, in the grocery store, while you're driving a car, when you can't sleep at night. Pray without ceasing.

TRIALS AND TRIBULATIONS

Help to make it happen

In the world you shall have tribulations: but be of cheer; I have overcome the world. (John 16:33)
That the trial of your faith, being much more precious than of gold that perishes, though it be tried with fire, might be found unto praise and honor and glory at the appearing of Jesus Christ. (1Peter 1:7)
Neither be you grieved; for the joy of the Lord is your strength. (Nehemiah 8:10)

I have to admit this one is a hard one for me and it always has been. The very idea of it sounds like an oxymoron. Years ago, one of my Bible teachers told me that spiritual maturity is sometimes attained through suffering. "Suffering"? I exclaimed. "I don't want to suffer!" And I meant it. We see in Job's experience that through trials and tribulations and suffering he grew to the point in his spiritual life where he could say to God, *"I have heard of You by the hearing of the ear, but now (after all these troubles) my eyes see You."* (Job 42:5) After reading Job we have to conclude that pain and suffering can be efficacious. But why is it so? Is it for suffering's sake alone? Remember the story of the old lady who was wailing and carrying on? Someone said to her, "What's the matter? Why are you so upset"? Her reply was, "God said in this world we would have tribulations and I am 'tribulating.'" She got the first part right, IN THIS WORLD YOU SHALL HAVE TRIBULATIONS (and notice it doesn't say if or maybe, it says you shall). But Jesus didn't tell us to "tribulate," but rather, *"Be of good cheer for I have overcome the world for you." (John 16:33).*

Oftentimes God uses adversity and trials to cleanse us and humble us in order to make us more like Jesus. As we go through this cleansing process, we will grow closer to God. Brother Lawrence said, "Therefore we should rejoice in our difficulties, bearing them as long as He wills, because only through such trials will our faith become purified."[33] Brother Lawrence didn't say God causes these adversities, he said God uses them to purify us.

I love the story of how a silversmith purifies silver. He boils the silver in a cauldron over very high heat. As he does, the impurities rise to the top of the cauldron. He skims them off and then cooks the silver again. Over and over, as the impurities rise, he skims them off. Someone asked him how he knew when the silver was ready and he could stop boiling it. His reply, "When I can see my face reflected in the silver." God also wants to see His reflection in us. He wants us to look like Him, without spot or blemish.

The reason that suffering makes us grow spiritually is because, when we experience problems, we are drawn close to God. In desperation we reach out to Him, we cling to Him because we know

---

[33] The Practice of the Presence of God, p 22

He is the one that can overcome for us. And because of this close proximity to Him, we are changed.

Through the years, I have learned that problems and trials are relative, like many other things. I was cleaning out a cabinet not long ago and among the notes and cards that I had saved, I found an old Sunday School lesson. On the front it said, "Trials and Tribulations." That piqued my interest, so instead of tossing it, I read it. The lesson was written almost 40 years ago, when my daughter, Mary Kathleen was a toddler. I said in the lesson (as an example of a trial) that I had gotten up that morning, gone downstairs to make breakfast for the children and opened a new box of oatmeal. Unfortunately, I knocked it over and it spilled all over the kitchen floor. Mary Kathleen was in the middle of it in the wink of an eye and I do believe she thought I did it just so she could play in it. Little did I know at that time, that as my children grew bigger, so would my trials and tribulations.

Earlier I said it's all relative. I recall a book, "The Long Walk."[34] The book is about six men who miraculously escaped from a horrendously cruel Russian prison camp in Siberia. After their escape they traveled a thousand miles from Siberia to India, which took them a year. They ate snakes to keep from starving, and they crossed the Himalayan mountains in the dead of winter, with nothing but moccasins on their feet. Comparing my life to theirs, I have never had a single problem in my whole life.

The reality is that I have. Looking back over the years, the bulk of my suffering has arisen through those I love the most, my children, my husband, and my friends. I believe that the extent of our human

---

34 The Long Walk by Slavomir Rawicz The Lyons Press, Guilford, CT, 1956

grief and suffering is directly measured by how much we love. If we didn't love, we wouldn't suffer. (I'm not referring to physical pain and suffering that we experience with surgery, cancer, etc). The most painful and grief-stricken experience I've ever had to go through was when my husband had open heart surgery. When he entered the hospital, my prayer was that he would be encircled by the manifest presence of God and that everybody that entered his room would walk into that circle of God's presence. As one of the doctors later told me, "Anything that could have gone wrong, did!" At first they opened his chest cavity to do the surgery. The next two times they opened his chest cavity was to stop the bleeding, but the fourth time his chest opened without provocation. We then had to get a plastic surgeon to put it back so that it wouldn't open again. One night, a few days after the plastic surgery, we anxiously waited for the doctor to come check on him and tell us whether he thought it would hold. The doctor was very late getting there. You could just feel the tension in the room. It was filled with pain, suffering, fatigue, and yes, fear, as we waited.(Fear is like a barracuda; it devours all hope and peace).

    I walked over to the bed and took my husband's hand and prayed: "Oh, Father, we need you so badly. Somehow I never knew that there could be so much pain, and suffering and fear in your manifest presence." Just as quickly as I spoke those words to Him, He gently spoke to me: "Anne, have you forgotten that I was crucified"? It was not what He said, but it was simply that He spoke. He was right there in that hospital room with us, walking through that valley of the shadow of death with us, giving us the strength to make it through. Knowing that He was in the middle of it all with us, gave us the courage and strength to endure.

Psalm 30:5 says: *Weeping may endure for a night, but joy comes in the morning.* That night, Joy didn't wait until morning He came in the middle of the night! I realized in that moment that joy is not the absence of suffering, but it is the presence of the Lord. *In his presence is the fullness of joy. Psalms 16:11*

Earlier I indicated that most of my trials and tribulations came from empathizing with others, but there was a time in my life that the trouble struck right in the center of my own heart. It was something that broke my heart and I just could not get over it, even trying as hard as I could. For weeks and months, I tried and prayed, and prayed and tried. It wouldn't go away no matter what I did. I talked to a friend, sought the help of a counselor many times, but to no avail. I was desperate. I decided to go to the beach alone. After spending much time in prayer with God, He delivered me from that pit. He is the very best counselor that we could possibly have. With God beside us, giving us His strength and courage, there are times when we just have to acknowledge, accept, and approve the bad things that happen to us, knowing that He is completely in control. With His help we can then just put on our hiking boots and climb over the mountain. Then it's behind us. That's the way it was with my problem. The most wonderful thing about it was, after God delivered me, He put a shield between me and that problem. And it never bothered me again. You know, sometimes counselors and friends can give us wrong advice (as did Job's friends). Jesus told us in John 14 that He would be our Counselor and our Comforter. Remember, there is no problem too big for Him.

When we experience a close, unbroken oneness with God, we can have a great abiding peace that sustains us even in the midst of difficulties. When my heart is troubled, I often repeat "Jehovah Shalom" (the peace of God) over and over. It has such a calming effect on my spirit. Once when my husband and I were traveling in Germany, we stayed in a hotel in Duesseldorf. When we walked into our room there was a feeling of heaviness and gloom. To get to sleep that night I kept repeating "Jehovah Shalom" to calm my spirit. Later, we found out that this hotel housed Nazis during the war. We must guard against any clouds of gloom, sadness, and darkness that could come between us and God. The only cloud we want is the cloud of God's Shekinah Glory to hover over us and lead us, as it did the Israelites of old.

I love what Brother Lawrence said about trouble: "When we practice being in God's presence the troubles that happen in the world can become like a blaze of straw that goes out even as it is catching fire."[35] To him the worst trial he could possibly imagine was losing his sense of God's presence with him.

A.B. Simpson, in his book, "Seeing the Invisible,"[36] said that man's extremity is God's own opportunity. That doesn't mean that God initiates the trials, but simply that, as we walk through them, God uses that opportunity to draw us to Him. I have always thought it so unfair when people blame God for bad things that happen. When my daughter was in college, one of her friends was killed in a boating accident. Everybody was in a state of shock and couldn't believe it happened. One of the most painful things they were struggling with was, Why did it happen? After much prayer and thought, I wrote the following article to comfort my daughter and her

---

35 The Practice of the Presence of God, p 68
36 Seeing the Invisible by A. B. Simpson   Wing Spread Publishers, Camp Hill, PA 1995

friends. (The local newspaper published it in the editorial section).

It's an age old question that everyone seems to ask when tragedy strikes – Why did it happen? Why? She, of all people didn't deserve it! Why? And, carried to its logical conclusion, it always ends with blaming God for such a hideous happening. Why did God cause it, let it happen, allow it? After much struggling and searching I'd like to share with you what I believe.

First of all, within the boundaries of "free will" that God has so graciously given us, there is an area that encompasses accidents (such as Annie's). God took a great big risk when He gave us free will, just as we as parents take big risks when we allow our children to drive cars, ride in boats, etc: for we know how often auto or boating accidents occur. But because we love, we allow, and take risks. Likewise, God. He didn't want to make us like robots, controlling our lives. Rather, He wanted us to be free, to be able to make choices – to go to the lake, let the wind blow through our hair, feel the exhilaration of skimming across the water on a beautiful sun-filled day. I believe that He receives great joy and pleasure from seeing us happy. Enjoying life to the fullest. I also believe that His heart breaks when accidents occur (like Annie's) and that He grieves infinitely more than we do. The reason He grieves more is because of His great and boundless love for each of us.

You see, the extent of our human grief and suffering is directly measured by the amount of love we have in our hearts for others. God, who is all love, has given us this capacity to reach out and love others as He loves us. As each of us has felt deep sorrow and grief for Annie because of our love for her, imagine if you will, the extent and scope of grief and suffering that He, who is all love, must feel!

So, putting all blame behind, wipe away the tears, hold your head up high and go forward to live life more fully than ever before – knowing that you possess that God-like love and compassion that has so recently surfaced. Go and share it with everyone you meet – while you have the chance. To love others is God's perfect will for each one of us. It is indeed our Utmost for His Highest!

Surprises

Help to make it happen

Living my life with God is so much fun, and I love it when He surprises me. One hot, summer morning at my new beach house, I arose early, made my coffee and went out on the deck to sit and drink it. I was still sleepy. When I heard the commotion down by the water, I was a bit confused. Seven or eight people were on the beach, jumping up and down in excitement and yelling: "Jubilee, Jubilee, it's a Jubilee!" I stood up to see why they were so excited. They were throwing nets into the water and when they pulled them to shore, the nets were full of shrimp, fish and crabs. One man had gigged a flounder and was proudly holding it up for the others to see! I ran in the house, grabbed a little crab net (the only thing I had) and scurried down to join in the fun. I was able to get shrimp by simply dipping the net in the water. I was handicapped (and frustrated) by not having anything but a small sand pail to put them in. But those shrimp were beautiful. In a store they would have been classified as jumbo shrimp! Then it was over before I could really grasp what had happened..

I went back into the beach house and called my daughter, who lives in Mobile and was married to a native Mobilian. I knew he could explain to me what a Jubilee was. I told him what had happened, nets full of shrimp, crab, and fish and that the people were yelling, "Jubilee!" I told him that I was able to catch shrimp with a crab net. "No," he said. "It's not a Jubilee, they only occur in Mobile Bay and in a remote bay in India. They've never had a Jubilee on the Gulf." He paused, then asked me if I had seen anybody with a flounder on a pike. When I told him that one man did have a flounder on a pike, he said, "I do believe you've had a Jubilee!"[37] (I later learned the Birmingham newspaper reported a Jubilee on Dauphin Island, the first they had ever heard of on the Gulf).

Our beach house had just recently been built, and I had gone there to put the finishing touches to it. The very next day, after the Jubilee, our minister came to bless the house. When he arrived I told him God had beaten him to it. He had blessed our house with a Jubilee! We named our house "La Place de Jubilee." I love it when God surprises me!

A couple of years after the Jubilee, my husband faced a difficult diagnosis. His doctor and all the other urologists at Grand Rounds who heard his case agreed he had renal carcinoma. His doctor told us we should get prepared and put things in order, because it was a most foreboding diagnosis. Of course, we were devastated. The children were at the beach house, so it was my job to go down there and break the news to them. When I boarded the plane, the tears that I had held back began to flow. I cried all the way to Mobile and then almost all the way to Dauphin Island. When I came to the very top

---

37   3 Jubilee is the name used locally for a natural phenomenon that occurs sporadically on the shores of Mobile Bay, a large body of water on Alabama's Gulf Coast. During Jubilee many species of crab and shrimp, as well as flounder, eels, and other demersal fish will leave deeper waters and swarm – in large numbers and very high density – in a specific area of the bay. A jubilee is a celebrated event in Mobile Bay, and it attracts large crowds, many drawn by the promise of abundant and easy-to-catch seafood. Although similar events have been reported in other bodies of water, Mobile Bay is the only place where the regular appearance of this phenomenon has been documented.

of that beautiful bridge I must cross over to get to Dauphin Island, God spoke to me. He said, "Remember Jubilee!" In that moment my tears of anguish were changed into an absolutely incredible faith. When I arrived at the beach house, all the children gathered round and I explained to them the diagnosis and what the doctors had said. I also told them how terribly upset I had been and how God spoke to me and calmed me down as I crossed the bridge. I told them that he said to me, "Remember Jubilee!" One of my daughters didn't understand, and my daughter-in-law, who was sitting next to her on the floor, turned to her and said, "God told her, 'Remember, you believe.'" **Remember Jubilee - Remember you believe.** In that room, instead of "surround sound," there was "Surround Faith." God had so empowered me with His faith that it spilled over onto my whole family!

Those that trust in the Lord, are like Mount Zion, which cannot be removed, but abides forever. As the mountains surround Jerusalem, so the Lord surrounds his people, from this time forth and forevermore. (Psalms 125:1-2 – NIV 2011)

The next week the doctors performed surgery on my husband as many, many people prayed for him. On the day of the surgery, my children, some friends, and I gathered in a hospital room awaiting the results. A phone in the room kept us abreast of what was going on in the operating room. The first call informed us that the surgery had started. On the second call, the nurse told us that they had sent a biopsy of the tumor to the laboratory. The third call informed us that the biopsy had come back negative and they were sending more of the tumor to the laboratory. The next call: biopsy negative, sending all of the tumor down to laboratory. When the phone rang next the nurse told my daughter, who had been answering the phone, that the doctor was getting ready to call and he wanted me to answer the phone. I picked up the phone when it rang. He told me that the tumor was benign. He apologized profusely for the original diagnosis and that he was sorry for all the anguish we had gone through.

The next day the surgeon who assisted with the operation told us that the tumor was the strangest looking tumor he had ever seen. I told him that I guess that's what they look like when God miraculously intervenes. Yes, I believe in miracles!

He gives us beauty for ashes, the oil of joy for mourning, the garment of praise for the spirit of heaviness. That we might be called trees of righteousness, the planting of the Lord, that He might be glorified. (Isaiah 61:3)

WORSHIP AND PRAISE
Help to make it happen

One of the best ways to connect us with God and to make us more acutely aware of His presence with us is by worshiping Him. I'm not speaking of our "worship service" on Sunday, but our own personal, one-on-one worship service. To worship God is to honor Him, to adore Him and to love Him with all our heart, mind, soul, and strength. Worship is a "direct connect." It plugs us in. Two of the most powerful tools in worship are praise and thanksgiving. These two are so closely knit it's difficult to separate them. Try it sometimes. Someone has aptly said worship is like a crown with two beautiful jewels. Those jewels are praise and thanksgiving.

One of the most beautiful expressions of spontaneous worship is found in Timothy 1:17. In this scripture Paul writes a letter to young Timothy. Suddenly, his heart bursts out in praise and honor to God. (And it wasn't even during his quiet time). Throughout the years, every time I read this verse, I can feel the praise vibrating from the page. *Now unto the King eternal, immortal, invisible, the only wise God, be glory and honor forever and ever. Amen*

Have you ever had moments like that? When your heart is just so full, so brimming over that you just can't keep it in a second longer? It happened to me one summer afternoon as I was driving into Crested

Butte, Colorado. It had been raining, but the rain had stopped and the sun was out. As I drove into the town, it was like driving into heaven.

The rain left an ethereal mist sitting over the city. The wildflowers covered the mountain sides and everything was so incredibly beautiful. I felt like falling on my face in awe and thanksgiving to our Great and Mighty and Incredible God. Those majestic mountains were such perfect evidence of His handiwork. We are told in Isaiah 40:10: *He can measure the mountains in His scales,* and I was in awe as I saw His power and might in those mountains.

As mentioned earlier, one very important reason we thank and praise God is because it brings us into His presence. Remember in Psalm 100 we are shown step by step how we can enter into His presence through thanksgiving and praise. We are ushered into His presence by praising and thanking Him. So, if you ever feel separated from God, try thanking and praising Him.

Philippians 4:6-7 gives us another reason why thanksgiving is so important. It plays a big role in bringing our prayers and concerns to God. *Be anxious for nothing, but in everything, through prayer and supplication with thanksgiving, let your request be known to God, And the peace of God, which passes all understanding, shall keep your hearts and minds through Christ Jesus.* Every prayer and every request must be made with thanksgiving. Thanksgiving is like an envelope in which we send our prayers to God.

We give thanks because God wants us to. Ephesians 5:20 reads: *Giving thanks always for all things unto God the father in the name of our Lord Jesus Christ.*

Do you remember the story of the lepers that Jesus healed? There were ten, but only one came back to thank Him: *And one of them, when he saw that he was healed, turned back, and with a loud voice glorified God, And fell down on his face at Jesus' feet giving Him thanks. And Jesus answering, said, Were there not ten cleansed? But where are the nine? (Luke17:15-17)*

We give thanks for all things, because He misses us when we don't thank Him.

We are also told to thank Him all the time. We begin in the morning, when our eyes open: *This is the day which the Lord has made; we will rejoice and be glad in it. (Psalm 118:24).* Our prayer can be as simple as "Thank you, Father, for this day You have given me. I invite You to be a part of every minute of it." Then, all during the day we spontaneously give Him thanks. When the day is done and we lie in our bed we enumerate all the blessings that He has poured out upon us and thank Him for each one. (Someone aptly said: When you can't sleep, count your blessings, not sheep!)

Some people stumble on the scripture in Ephesians 5:20: *Giving thanks always for all things unto God and the Father in the name of our Lord Jesus Christ.*

We can understand giving thanks for the good things, but *everything* includes the bad things too; like accidents, illnesses, hurricanes, etc. Some prefer the scripture in 1 Thessalonians 5:18: *In everything give thanks; for this is the will of God in Christ Jesus concerning you.*

I love the story about a 4 year-old boy whose parents were teaching him to give thanks before meals. They wanted him to say it spontaneously. Company came one night, and as they sat down for dinner, they asked the little boy to give thanks. "Oh no, do I have to"? was his response. Then, "O.K., I'll do it." With one eye closed and one eye open he proceeded to thank God for everything that came into that one-eyed vision. "Thank you, God, for the roast beef, the mashed potatoes, the green beans, the tomatoes, the iced tea, the salt and pepper, the knives and forks, and napkins." He then thanked God for all the people at the table, calling each one by name and he even thanked God for the dog under the table. When he finished, his brother said to him, "You thanked God for everything you saw, except that broccoli on your plate! Why didn't you thank Him for the broccoli? The little boy said, "Because I don't like broccoli!"

Sometimes we find things on our plate that we don't like and we don't thank God for them. We must remember that Romans 8:28 tells us: *All things work together for good to them that love God, to them who are the called according to His purpose.*

We do know that sometimes people don't seriously turn to God until broccoli shows up on their plates. So let's remember to thank Him for all things, or if you prefer, in *all* things! We must not let our feelings rob us of the privilege of thanking and praising Him. Sometimes our feelings will resist, rather than assist us, and that's when we offer the sacrifice of praise and thanksgiving.

It's fun to get in the habit of stopping during the day to praise and thank God. It takes only a moment. You can do it anywhere; at the grocery store, working in the yard or cooking dinner. I like to refer to these quick moments of praise as "Momentary Retreats." And God gives us so many visual aids to remind us to do this - just to stop and thank Him. One summer while my husband and I were in Charleston, we toured one of the river plantations. After we toured the home, we went to the blacksmith's quarters, and then on to the mill where they demonstrated how they made grits in the days gone by. As we left that building we walked out into a sunlit courtyard where a peacock was standing with his feathers spread in full glory! I just stood there in awe at what God had done. That peacock was such a beautiful, incredible manifestation of God's handiwork that it took my breath away. As humans, we grind corn, but God creates a peacock so perfectly symmetrical in color, in design and in every detail. What a humbling and awesome experience - what a "Momentary Retreat!! The Westminster Catechism condenses volumes of scriptural truth when it says: *The chief end of man is to glorify God and to enjoy Him forever.*[38] Praise and thanksgiving are indispensable parts of glorifying and relating to God. Through praise and thanksgiving we minister directly to Father God, Who ever seeks for us to worship Him.

---

38 The Westminster Catechism   (In 1643, English Parliament called upon learned, godly men to provide advice on worship, doctrine and discipline for the Church of England. They met at Westminster Abby and wrote the Catechism).

Take Off Your Shoes

PART V:
Conclusion

This is the Lord's doing;

it is marvelous in our eyes.

Psalm 118:23

The Butterfly Blessing

Behold, what manner of love the Father has bestowed upon us, that we should be called the children of God. (1ˢᵗ John 3:1)

I rebuilt our beach house, Jubilee, after Hurricane Katrina destroyed it. There was just enough beach left, and I was so excited that we were able to rebuild. To my dismay, the beach had become very susceptible to erosion, and, after a few minor hurricanes and multiple tropical storms, Jubilee was partially standing in the Gulf of Mexico. On calm days, which were rare, the water receded and we had a little beach in front of the house. But most of the time half the house was standing in water. During a storm one night water came rushing under the house. A tree lodged between the pilings under the house and, as the waves came crashing in, it sounded as if the house would fall into the sea. In that frightening moment I decided to move the house to higher ground. It was not an easy task, but after multitudinous trials and tribulations, the moving company was finally able to pull the house out of the water and carry it to a safe location, away from the Gulf.

After moving it, our first task was to build another set of stairs in front of the house, which was previously in the water. After completing the steps, we had to paint them. Because I didn't know which parts of the stairs to paint, I drove around the island looking at various houses that had similar stairs. I found what I was looking for. A house on the bayside of the island had stairs similar to ours. It also had a "for sale" sign in front of it, and it looked abandoned. I pulled into the driveway, got out of my car and walked around the house. I walked up the back stairs, knocked on the door, but as I had guessed, no one was there. I sat on the swing on the back porch, overlooking a spectacular view of the bay, and I have never felt a more tangible peace in my life. It was one of those "God Moments" or "Momentary Retreats." As I left the house, I got the number of the real estate agent on the sign in the yard. When I returned to the beach house I told my son I had just been to a house that screamed peace. He said, "But Mom, that's an oxymoron." I didn't care. After the tumultuous months of wind, water, unrest and problems, this house was a solace for my troubled soul and it did scream peace!

I put Jubilee up for sale and bought the house that my son jokingly named, "Screaming Peace." The first time I went to the house after I bought it, I drove into the driveway. When I left the car, there were hundreds of monarch butterflies flying around. I had never seen anything like it. I was standing in a wonderland! Not only were there butterflies in the air (they looked like flying flowers), but the limbs of the trees and bushes were laden with them. There were so many that it looked like the trees and bushes were "afire" with God. This was definitely a "take off your shoes and throw them in the air" kind of moment. In times like this I need a witness. I called my daughter who lives in Mobile and said, "Can you come out immediately and bring your camera. This is something you and Joshua (my grandson) have got to see." When she arrived, I told her that God was blessing the house with butterflies. This blessing is symbolic of how extravagant God is in His love for us. It also made me realize the great lengths to which He will go to get our attention so He can spend time with us. He ever waits to pour his love and blessings upon each one of us, and

He patiently waits for us to open our eyes to see Him and our hearts to receive Him.

Postscript: After the Butterfly Blessing we named the house "Monarch," but its nickname will always be "Screaming Peace."

Father God, For each one who reads this book I pray that You will put such a hunger in their hearts for You that it will not be satisfied until they have found You in a viable, dynamic way. I pray that as they live, move and have their being in You that they will be aware of Your presence with them every minute of every day. As they open the doors of their hearts to invite You in, may You bless them exceedingly and abundantly far more than they could possibly hope or imagine. Amen

Take Off Your Shoes

AFTERTHOUGHT

Way out of my reach

When I first read "Abide in Christ" the following passage was so lofty, so for out of my reach that I couldn't even begin to grasp it - but God kept pulling me back to it. I would go back and read it again and again and it seemed to cling to me. I had the feeling that God was trying to tell me something - to help me understand something so exalted that my brain just couldn't fathom it.

The soul need but have one care – to abide closely, fully, wholly in Christ Jesus. Abiding in Him, you receive of Him His Spirit of love and compassion toward sinners, making you desirous to seek their good. By nature the heart is full of selfishness. Even in the believer, his own salvation and happiness are often too much his only object. But abiding in Jesus, you come into contact with His infinite love; its fire begins to burn within your heart; you see the beauty of love; your learn to look upon loving and serving and saving your fellow-men as the highest privilege a disciple of Jesus can have. Abiding in Christ, your heart learns to feel the wretchedness of the sinner still in darkness, and the fearfulness of the dishonor done to your God. With Christ you begin to bear the burden of souls, the burden of sins not your own. As you are more closely united to Him, somewhat of that passion for souls which urged Him to Calvary begins to breathe within you, and you are ready to follow His footsteps, to forsake the heaven of your own happiness, and devote your life to win the souls Christ has taught you to love.[39]

Into the Cedar Grove Friendship House, where I taught a weekly Bible Class, came five young men, each with stockings pulled tightly over the top of their heads. I was not afraid, but I was not comfortable. Gangs are rampant in this area of town, and I knew what evil things they were capable of doing. However, I remembered I was the one who had asked that we fervently pray for the "gangs" when we had our city-wide crusade. After a couple of Bible classes I realized that I needed someone, beside myself, to come into the class and speak to these new students. I asked a young minister that I knew and he came and did an excellent job. He began his lesson by asking the students about their hopes and dreams. Each spoke up saying what they wanted to do in life. I remember one said he wanted to be a barber and another said he had always wanted to be a truck driver. He then told them about Jesus and how it was possible that He could help make those dreams come true. As the class was coming to an end the minister asked everyone to bow their heads and close their eyes. He then proceeded to do an "Alter Call" much like I had seen Billy Graham do. He asked those who wanted to receive Christ into their lives to raise their hands. He said a prayer and told us we could open our eyes. He then asked those who had raised their hands to come up and stand with him. All five of the gang members went forward. As the minister spoke to them, God spoke to me. He

---

39 Abide in Christ by Andrew Murray, pp 130, 131 Whitaker House, Springdale PA 1979.

said, "Anne, do you know how much I love you"? My reply, "Yes, Lord, I do and I thank you so much for loving me." He then told me to look at the young men and I did. They seemed like the "rejects" of society: worn out tennis shoes, dirty tee-shirts, tattered jeans and somewhat of a desperate look on each of their unshaven faces. And wearing stockings on their heads (for goodness sakes!) As I sat there contemplating them, God interrupted my train of thought and gently said to me, "Each one of these young men is a special treasure to me. They are like precious jewels and I love them so much." I can't even begin to describe how I felt in that moment except I knew I was in the Presence of God and with tears streaming down my face (Joy, joy, joy, tears of joy!), He gave me the awesome privilege of glimpsing into His heart of love. A love so beautiful and extravagant that it left me weak and limp. Oh! How He loves you and me. Oh! How He yearns for all of us to be nestled under His wings of love. And as that lofty passage says, *as we abide in Him He fills us with that same kind of love and compassion.* A love so profound that it reaches for and beyond our human abilities and imaginations.

Will I ever get there? It does seem impossible in my lifetime. But if it ever happens, I truly need what Andrew Murray said - *the fire of God to burn within my heart.* Pray that I get there.

Prayer: Thank you God for being a God of Love and Grace. Let your love and grace burn within our hearts. Amen

Shoe Therapy

Shoe Therapy

How To Live As A Confident Christian Woman By Putting Your Best Foot Forward

Lenora Nazworth

Shoe Therapy

Foreword

A few years ago, my travels took me to a writing conference in Dallas, Texas. I was a new novelist, unsure about the path I was on and seeking guidance. With uncertainty, I sat down at a breakfast table, feeling as out of place as flip-flops at a formal dance.

With a room full of tables and many familiar colleagues to visit with, a woman with a beautiful and welcoming smile chose to sit down next to me. In that moment, with that small gesture, she made my way easier.

As we started to introduce ourselves, I looked at her more closely, and she looked at me. Turns out, we lived only a few miles from one another in Shreveport and had crossed paths before. And, turns out, she would become my mentor and friend in the years ahead, offering the kind of inspiration she gives in these pages.

That gracious writer was Lenora Worth, (Lenora Nazworth) and I know God brought her to me that day. She stepped in – wearing nice shoes! – and guided me through the intricacies of becoming a professional novelist. Along the way she taught me a lot about how to live with a generous and persistent spirit.

Lenora's essays here reflect the spirit by which she lives her life. She moves forward step by step, with dedication and discipline. She loves to have fun and knows how to work hard. She exudes faith and friendship.

The journey of life takes us in many directions, and we need wisdom and companions for our travels. In these pages, Lenora uses the symbol of everyday shoes to talk about how God walks with us and how we can make a difference in the lives of others. She takes a lighthearted approach to a deep subject and helps us think about spiritual issues in new ways for our everyday walk.

She reminds us to be faithful and to keep our footing with God. She nudges us to trust and obey.

In my life, God has led me onto paths I would never have expected and has sent me people like Lenora Nazworth and Anne Wilson to encourage and inspire me every step of the way. Each of these women reminds me that we are called to use our gifts and to help make our corner of the world a better place.

Put your feet up and enjoy their fresh perspective. You'll be glad you walked with them on this journey.

Travelling mercies, wherever your shoes lead you …

~Judy Christie

INTRODUCTION

Most women love shoes. Maybe because picking out the right pair of shoes makes our day start out better. When our shoes match our outfit and feel good on our feet and look good in the mirror, we have a better attitude and we can march out the door feeling confident about ourselves. Isn't it the very same with faith and prayer, too?

If we start our day with the right attitude, based on the precious passages we can find in the Bible, we become fully dressed in the armor of God's love.

But how do we accomplish this kind of confidence in today's world? Is it really all about the shoes? Or could it also be about wearing the proper wardrobe from head-to-toe, starting with our mindset?

Are you ready to step out in style and grace? Are you ready for a little shoe therapy? Let's get going!

Shoe Therapy

Mary Janes—Prim, Proper and Petrified

Then you will walk safely in your way,

and your foot will not stumble.

Proverbs 3:23

Do you remember Buster Brown? He was a pretty famous cartoon character created in 1902 by Richard Felton Outcault. When a sales executive for the Brown Shoe Company bought the rights to the Buster Brown name, a whole new brand began. But what most people don't realize is that Buster's little sister Mary Jane had an even greater impact on shoes. Dear little Mary Jane wore black strapped shoes and started a foot wear revolution that is still going strong today. She's the inspiration behind the Mary Jane style.

Think back to when you were little. You probably owned pair of black patent shoes with a dainty little strap that buckled across the top of your foot. You might have practiced learning to buckle those shoes all on your own. And you probably didn't realize that was your very first step toward becoming a strong, confident woman. Forget learning to tie your shoes! Buckling a Mary Jane strap was big business back then. It combined the charm of little girl cuteness with the very serious desire to do things on your own.

That's because Mary Janes give us an attractive little-girl look, but they allow us to have big girl dreams. They're pretty without being too frilly. They're sensible without being to staid. Mary Janes represent our childhood memories combined with our goals and objectives in the here and now.

Even if your knees are shaking, you can have confidence in a pair of Mary Janes. And that is exactly the kind of confidence Christ can give us, too. Just like a pair of good Mary Janes, the love of Christ gives us the strength to buckle up and get on with things. And God's love also gives us the sturdy support we need in order to march out into the world with a mature attitude and the ability to get things done.

Whether you wear your Mary Janes flat and casual or kitten-heeled and sleek, you'll find this is the one shoe that never lets a girl down. You can go from taking baby steps to strutting right out the door with style, armored in God's grace and love. And a proper pair of shoes.

Sneakers—Tiptoes, Temptation and Tenacity

'The time has come,' the walrus said, *'to talk of many things: of shoes and ships - and sealing wax - of cabbages and kings.'*

Lewis Carroll

People like to walk. Research shows that the average person walks about 2,000 miles per year. And women are now told to try and get in about 10,000 steps per day. No wonder we love our sneakers! The Ked, introduced in 1917, was one of the very first sneakers. Before then, sneakers were little more than "croquet shoes". But the sensibleness of sneakers has become a marketing machine, with designs now consisting of everything from women's exercise shoes to athletic men's shoes. In-between, we have runners, cross-trainers, gym shoes, yoga socks and Earth shoes. But Nike's "Just Do It" campaign was already in play with women long before any big name athletics did commercials for the brand.

Women learn how to just get on with things at an early age. Children, work, husbands, volunteer work and other duties demand our attention every day. We can multi-task in our sneakers, our feet barely hitting the floor. (Nike, by the way, is named for the Greek goddess of victory.) While she had wings, we do not. Thus, we have sneakers that allow us to walk on air.

But our sneakers can also allow us to tiptoe over certain confrontations or mow down certain obstacles. Maybe we don't want to take a stand so we waffle along, meandering through our days. Or maybe we think just because we have on winged shoes, we can resist temptation or even give in to temptation. So what, we'll walk off that worry, right? Then we realize we're just too tired to walk off anything—food, worry, denial—just about anything. But putting on a good sensible, comfortable pair of sneakers does help us to strengthen our muscles, both our physical bodies and our spiritual muscles. We don't have to hide from God's word and we don't have to sneak around in fear. Christ gives us a gentle foot-bed on which to stand and walk, even when we're too tired to take that next step. We can get in shape, stand strong and resist temptation if we put on a good pair of sneakers, along with the attitude that yes, we can do anything with God's guidance.

Mules–Mad, Manipulative and Mindless

If I have learned one thing in this life, it is that God will not tie my shoes without me.

Doug Boyd

I still have my feet on the ground, I just wear better shoes.

Oprah Winfrey

Women are known for being stubborn. That goes for the kind of shoes we wear, too. Take mules, for example. The mule is not that complicated. It is basically a sole with one big strip of leather across the vamp. Mules can be open-toed or closed in, but they are always backless and strapless and come in various shapes and forms such as clogs or sandals. They can be casual or dressy, with low-heels or platforms. But at the end of the day, a good mule is easy to slip on and a delight to wear.

But the mule is a tenacious shoe.

It dates back to ancient times and gets its name from the Latin word <u>mulleus</u>. A mulleus was a type of fancy shoe worn in ancient Rome, usually by government officials. While the mulleus was considered an impractical luxury in Roman times, it proved to become popular and eventually became a favorite of European royalty.

Okay, so the mule isn't the most practical shoe and its name has no relation to pack mules, but it does teach women a little bit about life. Today, mules reflect our instant gratification society. We can put them on and go or toss them off very quickly when we've had enough. Today's styles even allow for changing out the strap on the same shoe, to fit the color or mood!

When life gets bumpy, we do tend to slip and slid right out of our stride, so to speak. We get mad with life, so we tend to want to manipulate our circumstances in a mindless way. But it's not any fun, slipping and sliding right out of our convenient easy-to-slip-on mules.

Sometimes it's just better to kick off those old mules and stand still, so we can listen to God and give the control over to Him. If we allow God to help us find our way, we can let go and get over being mad and mindless and wanting everything our way—and right now.

After all, a good pair of mules just means we're willing to relax and let go a bit. Not always practical but still sometimes necessary in order to find the right path.

God doesn't want us to slip and slid and He doesn't always show us the most convenient avenue. So don't be mulish when you're slipping on those mules, honey. Wear your mules with style instead of stubbornness. Let God's grace keep you on solid footing.

Boots–Cozy, Covered and Courageous

One must always have one's boots on and be ready to go.

Michel de Montaigne

Technically, a boot isn't actually a shoe because it covers not only the foot, but the ankle and leg too. Boots were created to be functional, to keep out the elements and protect the wearer. But those days have changed. Boots started centuries ago with Genghis Khan and his hand-made, wooden-heeled red boots and went on to find the Duke of Wellington. That's where the famous Wellingtons got their name. These manly leather boots were a snap to construct out of four easy pieces. So easy, they were used in the Civil War. And they are still popular today.

Now boots are fashionable as well as functional. Anything from Doc Martens and Uggs to Jimmy Choo Victorians or Michael Kors ankle-length can qualify as a boot these days. Short and clunky or tall with spiked heels, boots are here to stay.

Remember Nancy Sinatra singing "These boots are made for walking." She sung that song during the 1960s, a time when women were discovering they could be equal and sure-footed but still feminine and stylish. It seemed to be a rally cry for American women, telling them they could have it all. But women do need to be "tough as old boots" in how they carry on and multi-task in ways that would impress even a crusty old cowboy.

Now boots have moved from the days of the wild West and cowboys to the mean streets of New York's Fifth Avenue and beyond. Now we have fashion boots, sports boots, work boots, short boots, long boots, and cowboy boots so fancy that a hardworking Texan wouldn't dare be caught dead in them.

Boots give us a cozy feeling. We're all tucked in and safe in our boots. They cover us when the weather is horrible and they make us courageous as we go marching to the principal's office to discuss our child's latest escapade. After all, we all have a bit of the warrior in us, red boots or not. If we use that strength to pull ourselves up by our bootstraps, we will become stronger in our faith. We are covered from the storms and battles of life by the insulation and warmth of God's protective love. Those four easy pieces--Scripture, Prayer, Compassion and Forgiveness—just like boots, allow us to hide a multitude of sins. Christ is like our favorite sheepskin lined boots—warm and comforting and never out of style. Wearing a good pair of boots is just part of our spiritual armor. And ... it's an adventure!

Slippers—Resting, Regrouping and Resilient

*To be happy, it first takes being comfortable …
in your own shoes. The rest can work up from there.*

Sophia Bush

Sometimes, we just have to be still and rest. That is where our slippers come in. Slippers are soft and lightweight, as in "Take a load off." Known as "house shoes", slippers bring us soothing relief and comfort. They are easy to slip into and out of. And … they can make us feel better simply because sometimes slippers can be goofy. Anyone ever had a pair of bunny slippers? Or maybe a pair of oversized furry slippers? These lazy, easy shoes also come in bright colors to lift our spirits.

The first slippers were probably more like moccasins, soft and made of animal skins in suede or leather. Today, most are made from those two materials as well as cotton or wool, rubber and mocleather. Which only adds to the adornments of fur and funny, fuzzy characters. Now, we even had slipper socks so we can go sliding across the floor like ice skaters.

While the slipper's complete history is rather mysterious, we can agree that wearing our favorite house shoes just makes our feet happy and our attitude full of gratitude. It's no secret that most working women kick off their pumps and put on their fuzzy slippers the minute they get home.

We start out in slippers. A baby's tiny feet can only handle so much and soft warm slippers bring comfort to growing infants. These days, college students are apt to wear slippers to class—gasp! And while Dorothy had her ruby slippers and Cinderella had her glass slippers, women today don't have to go to such extremes to find comfort and security. Slippers let us slip into our upper room and find some peace while we tell the Lord all of our triumphs and troubles.

It's okay to have fuzzy slippers and it's a lot better than having fuzzy logic. Let your happy feet show some character and laugh at yourself every now and then. Like Dorothy said, "There is no place like home." Especially if you can wear your favorite pair of comfy slippers.

No matter what type of shoes you wear, remember the true beauty you possess can shine through in God's abiding love. Christ is always there, walking with us. Even if we are barefoot.

Do not let your adornment be merely outward--arranging the hair, wearing gold, or putting on fine apparel -- rather let it be the hidden person of the heart, with the incorruptible beauty of a gentle and quiet spirit, which is very precious in the sight of God. 1 Peter 3:3-4 (NKJV)

*Loafers—Laid-back,
Learning, and Laughing at Life*

How beautiful are the feet of those

who bring good news.

Romans 10:15

From the Bass Weejun to the Belgian loafer, these shoes make a statement while they hardly make a sound. Loafers are the laid-back cousins of the shoe family. They can be a bit high-browed and are often coveted by the chic crowd because while they are sensible, they are also called "moc-casual". Loafers represent slippers—or moccasins--and are made to be as comfortable as house shoes, even if women prefer to wear them for shopping and lunch.

Worn by everyone from James Dean to JFK, loafers hit the United States in the 1930's and have evolved into a classic that is now mostly worn by prep school students and PTA moms. But a lot of people in-between love loafers, too.

You might think of "penny" loafers and wonder why a penny? Actually, someone smart thought the little slits called lips on the loafers vamp would make a good place to put a dime—the amount it cost to use a pay phone back in the day. (You do remember pay phones, right?) Anyway, another person who wanted a bit of shine changed his loose change to a penny and put that in his shoe. And that's how the penny loafer became so famous.

But while the lowly loafer might sound casual, it's actually more of a work horse since this shoe started with Norwegian dairy farmers—and Bass Weejuns took that one step further by naming their famous loafers after those farmers.

All of those preppy school kids have the right idea when they put on their loafers. There is something to be said about being prepared, whether it's for college or whether it's for life.

Christ offers us our own "phone home" and we don't even have to put a penny in our shoes. If we walk in the word of God, we won't loaf around as is we're lost. We can put on comfortable shoes and still have enough gumption to call out to a higher source.

Whether we choose to wear our loafers with jeans or a suit, we should wear them with the comfort of Christ hidden away like a shiny penny. It will come in handy with each step we take. No phone booth needed.

*Walking Shoes—Wary,
Weary and Worldly*

Few people know how to take a walk. The qualifications are endurance, plain clothes, old shoes, an eye for nature, good humor, vast curiosity, good speech, good silence and nothing too much.

Ralph Waldo Emerson

Thousands of years ago, walking made things easier for humans. It was a good way to get from one place to another. Soldiers often went barefoot but fully armored into war. Many hundreds of years later, long distance walkers in Europe and America earned a lot of money, simply by walking fast and far.

Then in 1877, Mary Marshall walked about fifty miles in twelve hours. She had to have been tired when she finished. But today, most women probably already walk a lot further than that in one day (and we're encouraged to walk at least 10,000 steps). Women and walking shoes just go hand-in-hand. We wear our walking shoes to the mall and get in a good workout while window shopping. Or we can put on our walking shoes and help paint a house or rebuild a village.

Walking for sport and exercise is now so popular that a new and improved walking shoe shows up on a weekly basis. The thing about walking shoes—they have a more flexible sole than regular shoes. And they have these tiny air holes to keep the walker cool, calm and collected. Even when she's huffing and puffing and trying to make it to the finish line. And we all know there is more than one kind of finish line out there. Walking shoes are the plow horses of the shoe world.

Whether our walking shoes have a kinetic foot bed such as the Earth shoe, or a wobbly bottom such as the Fit-Flops and Skeechers Shape-Ups, we should know that a good walk can bring us closer to God. Walking and praying allows <u>us</u> to have a more flexible soul and we can take in some fresh air and get rejuvenated by breathing and praying. (That's probably why God gave us our own air holes.)

No matter your path, you need the proper equipment and the proper perspective. Get closer to God's touch on a long path through a tree-shaded park or a hefty hike up a stone-faced mountain. So don't be so straight-laced and prissy, missy. Get on a pair of good walkers and take off on a new adventure. That old saying from Lao-Tzu, "A journey of a thousand miles starts with a single step" completely applies to walking shoes. Battered, tattered, muddy and grimy, they keep on working in the same way God's love keeps on working on us. We can go from wary to weary to worldly in a twelve minute mile.

Wedges—Worried, Wondering and Wandering

A man cannot make a pair of shoes rightly unless he does it in a devout manner.

Thomas Carlyle

Sometimes you just need a little support. This is where the trusty and sturdy wedge comes in. This always popular shoe came into fashion in the 1930s. Height was all the rage and the wedge offered a solution to this and also matched those famous big-shouldered dresses and suits that were all the rage.

In 1935, Salvatore Ferragamo created an orthopedic wedge and then one with more of a heel. He used cork and wood since there was a leather shortage during World War II. Sometimes a wedge could go to five inches high. And these shoes are still high and popular today, because they give women height and support.

The wedge has a lot to offer. First, wedges come in all sizes and shapes, and in fabrics from floral to leather to crocheted lace. The wedge is sturdy and dependable and not as hazardous at some other tall sandals. The wedge offers us a platform, a place to stand tall but still feel balanced. The sole is thick and made of only one piece of material.

And the name is pretty telling. Sometimes we can get wedged into situations or predicaments that make us feel off balance and a bit trapped. But a sturdy espadrille shoe with a pretty floral strap can give us strength to carry on. We might be worried, we might wonder what comes next, or maybe we're just wandering around trying to find that much needed platform from which to shout, but the wedge, just like the strength of our faith, can give us balance and support.

We have a platform on which to stand. It's called God's love. But it sure doesn't hurt to stand tall in a pretty pair of shoes whenever we discover that we have the strength inside to stop worry, wondering, or wandering and step up to the mike. With each step we take, we become stronger in God's grace. Isn't it nice to know you can become centered and sure if you lean on those sturdy wedges and take that first step toward a stronger faith and a solid platform?

Wedges are thick-skinned. Women can be that way, too.

So tie up those ribbons and wear those espadrilles.

Your shoes will survive and so will you.

*Flip Flops—Flustered,
Fatigued and Famished*

Let a little water, I pray you, be fetched, and wash your feet, and rest yourselves under the tree.

Genesis 18:4

Flip-flops are one of the oldest forms of footwear. From ancient Egypt to Japan to New Zealand to the Americas and beyond, some form of flip-flops has been around for close to 6,000 years.

Flip-flops represent a more casual, laid-back life. Practical and simple, they consist of a bottom and two straps and are called everything from thongs to Zories to slip-slaps. And they've been worn by everyone from peasants and soldiers to surfers and surgeons. Flip-flops are used in colleges and army camps as a way to avoid germs and bacteria in showers and sleeping quarters. They were originally made from papyrus leaves, rawhide, wood, straw and even the yucca plant, but today they consist of leather and plastic.

Flip-flops might seem flimsy, but these hardworking shoes are pretty sturdy. They can handle water, sand, mud and even shopping malls. They became popular in the United States in the early 1950s and have remained a staple in the shoe world to the tune of $2 billion annually. That's a lot of slip-slaps.

Like any good thing, they can be worn too much and might just cause a few foot problems. But if you're weary and famished, flip-flops can get you to the nearest watering hole or casual restaurant. These days, they are grudgingly accepted even at the White House. Flip-flops are like chameleons; they can change with the tide and go from easy and casual to dressy and sparkling. Keep in mind that flip-flops do make noise.

Others might not tell we're exhausted and floundering around, but God hears us flip-flopping along, lost on the path to paradise. Sometimes, even with a good pair of shoes, we're afraid to take that next step. But God walks that journey with us and his flip-flops are sturdy and sure. We don't need to flitter around or fall flat on our face as we travel over the mountains and valleys of life. Christ has on his flip-flops and he's right there with us.

*High heels—Tall,
Tittering and Traditional*

Shoe Therapy

Funny that a pair of really nice shoes make us feel good in our heads - at the extreme opposite end of our bodies.

Levende Waters

Women love their high heels. Stilettos, some are called. Does the name Manolo Blahnik ring a cash register bell with you? Mr. Blahnik has made high heels an art form. He creates one of a kind masterpieces that made women swoon and make men weep (when they get the bill.)

And what is it about a well-heeled shoe that has all of us rushing off to the nearest department store clearance sale, anyway?

For one thing, they give us a certain power. Named after a certain knife for their slender heels, stilettoes give us a sense of adventure and romance. We feel more important in high heels. We're taller. We feel like Cinderella after the prince brings her that missing shoe. Everything just seems to fit perfectly. From the Egyptians to members of the French court (both men and women) high heels have been around for centuries. These slender heeled beauties became a status symbol long before New York fashion models got sore feet.

And speaking of sore feet—if it looks too good to be true but wears like a torture chamber, then you'd better understand that high heels can sometimes be too much of a good thing. They mirror the temptations we have in life.

But then, any guilty pleasure is that way, isn't it?

Wearing these works of art too long can lead to all sorts of foot problems and … they can even damage floors because your foot has to extend a lot of pressure with each step. These shoes might hold your heart, but they truly will make your feet ache.

It's important to understand that the highest of heels have a core of steel to support your weight on that tiny, tiny stem. And that core, darlings, is the good part of your beloved high heel. Because even when you're tittering on improper shoes Christ is stronger than that core of steel that supports you along the way. Women wearing high heels is a time-honored tradition. Women turning to Christ to find their inner core of steel is also a time-honored tradition. It's not so much the shoes you wear as the walk you walk. Keep Christ at the center and you will stand tall. Keep the traditions that you value and you will have a bargain each time you put on those Cinderella beauties and head out with your prince. You don't have to be a femme fatale to be a strong, well-heeled woman.

*Pumps—Empowered,
Encouraged, Energetic*

For we walk by faith, not by sight.

2 Corinthians 5:7

Pumps have been called "the little black dress" of shoes. And with good reason. Somewhere between a flat and a stiletto, pumps are the working girl's dream shoe. They are elegant, classic and feminine, even though in the 16th century, they were also worn mostly by stuffy old footmen. The word "pump" is from poumpe. Apparently, that was the sound of these shoes (worn by men) hitting the polished royal floors back then. As the power of the pump progressed through the ages, women claimed this smashing shoe as their own. Jackie O made pumps a must-have for any well-heeled woman. Throw on a pair of pearls and some pumps and you become empowered.

Working women everywhere have always rejoiced in the pump. This fashionable but sensible shoe keeps women from getting carried away, but allows them to be creative and quirky, too. It's a good balance between "bad girl" and "goody-two-shoes". Pumps can be plain and simple or embellished and fancy, so they suit the many moods of being a woman. You can wear a pair of black kitten heels to the office and at five o'clock, pull out a couple of clip-on squares of brocade and sequins and attach those to the vamp then … walk out the door ready for dinner and a night on the town.

Pumps, like women, know how to multi-task with speed and style. They show us that we can be empowered if we know a few rules of the game. And like our friends, they encourage us to keep moving, to step forward toward good works and helping others. These pretty, interesting shoes give women energy. Not to mention they work with everything from city shorts and a nice blouse to jeans and a long sweater. And they really shine with a cocktail dress!

Pumps are the go-to shoe. And don't we all need something like that in our closets? That is how God is in our lives, a staple, always there when we need to go to our upper room and be alone, always there when we're multi-tasking and going through the stress of the day. Pumps bring women into the adult world of everyday routine. But they are never boring and routine. And neither is God's love for us. His love gives us the perfect empowerment.

Sandals—Sand, Sea and Satisfaction

All God's children need traveling shoes.

Maya Angelou

Not to be confused with their laid back cousin, the flip-flop, sandals bring a certain sophistication to an open air foot. Sandals have been around since forever. They come in many forms and shapes and have changed a bit since the days of killing dinosaurs or walking through the desert. An ideal sandal will leave most of your upper foot exposed so that your whole foot can breathe a little easier and your poor toes get to see the sunshine.

Another good thing about sandals—they require less material so they are less expensive to make. (So you can have a pair in every color and shape.) And they come in many colors and shapes in the world of fashion. While sandals were very popular in Egypt and Greece in the good old days, they seemed to disappear for thousands of years. In the 1920s when so many new things came along, so did sandals. Again. Someone figured out how to make them high-heeled and the rest is fashion history. Today, we all love a good pair of fabulous Gladiator sandals. But we don't have to fight lions to wear them.

Sandals started out as flats with straps but they now leap into high heel mode with a slender heel and a sparkling strap. Prom queens love to wear bejeweled sandals underneath their satin and tulle gowns. Sandals pair nicely with skirts and shorts, jeans and trousers or a pretty summer sundress. They can move from the beach to the ballet in record time, too. And all the while, your feet are happy to be part of the walking world. Open air living makes feet smile. So if you like to "walk like an Egyptian" in your Birkenstocks or your Skeechers, sandals are the shoe for you. Dressy or casual, sandals can walk the walk.

The best thing about sandals—they remind us of how Jesus walked the earth in his sturdy sandals, his robes flowing, his presence as warm and comfortable as our favorite pair of huaraches. Christ brings us that type of comfort, the kind that conjures up sand and sea and a sense of love and contentment. Every now and then, we have to trust in that image of the Lord walking through the sand.

And know that we need to keep our sandals planted firmly on the ground, because he is always right there, walking with us.

Shoe Therapy